THE FILTH AMENDMENT

THE FILTH
AMENDMENT

Rushton versus Sextremes
★ **William Rushton** ★

Queen Anne Press
Macdonald & Co · London and Sydney

© William Rushton 1981

First published in 1981 by Queen Anne Press, a division of
Macdonald & Co (Publishers) Ltd, Holywell House,
Worship Street, London, EC2A 2EN

Illustrations by William Rushton

ISBN 0362 00555 9

Typeset in Great Britain by Cylinder Typesetting, London
Printed and bound in Great Britain by Waterlow and Sons Ltd,
Dunstable

CONTENTS

Introduction   6

In The Beginning Was That Word   9

The Original Sin   14

When They Began to Beget   20

The Origin of the Specious   24

The Greeks   28

The Romans   36

The Dark Ages   41

The Vikings   45

The Wit and Wisdom of the Lord Chamberlain   47

The View From Behind the Net Curtains   50

Death of a Hero   53

The Age of Chivalry   56

The Virgin Queen   59

Christmas 1984   63

The British in India   66

Everything You Ever Wanted to Know about Sex and
Never Knew Existed   74

Oliver Cromwell, Protector   78

Some Cautionary Words of a Medical Nature   82

In Good King Charles' Golden Days   84

The War of Independence   88

Queen Victoria Dead – A Nation Mourns   92

INTRODUCTION

I wouldn't be writing this book if Mrs White-house hadn't popped the question. And a strange question it was, too; not one you would pop in the norm unless perhaps you were deeply into nostalgia. (Of a sudden I'm thinking to myself there's a million-seller in *The Sexual Antics of an Edwardian Country Gentlewoman,* but I digress.)

I was standing at the bookstall on Euston station, searching hard for a book with a cover seemly enough to be borne north on British Rail, when I first saw the query working its eyebrows at me from a shelf. *Whatever Happened to Sex?* it asked. In shiny red letters on black, like a blousy houri in a low bar on the front at Port of Spain. Had I not seen Mother Whitehouse's name emblazoned above it, I might well have supposed that the second question would read 'Like a nice time, sailor?'

'Whatever happened to sex?' is a daft question at best. 'Whatever happened to shirt-tails?' is more pertinent. Or window-cleaners? Whatever happened to Brilliantini and his Music of the Motorways? (For me music died when the last '78' went out the window.) What sadness befell Trumble Hurll, the Vomiting Baritone? Good questions these, each de-manding an answer. Sex, as far as I can gather – and I am but a layman – is still alive and kicking, both for and against the pricks.

I remember thinking at the time that, if any-one should have an answer, 'tis Mother White-house as she must know a lot more about it than I do. She has it rammed down her throat daily, insofar as if she is not personally manning her control panel like Ming-the-Merciless – stiff with computers, warning hooters and screens – then her minions are reporting to her every

hour on the hour the view from behind their seedy net curtains. Big Sister is Watching You.

In fairness, I must say that I find Mother Whitehouse's gestures and posturings no more or less offensive than the spastic gyrations of a flaccid, elderly bump-and-grinder revealing all to the music of our times in a Soho sub-basement.

Ye Gods, now I think about it, I'm a centrist. Not in the political sense; though I feel we owe a small debt of thanks to those who have hurled their neat trilbies into the middle, leaving us at last with two political parties that finally disagree on the main issues. But when it comes to a choice between the dull glow of the Festival of Light and the gloom of the black hole of *Oh, Calcutta,* I find myself firmly planted there in the middle of the road, traditional last resting-place of the two-dimensional hedgehog.

Years ago I was giving Dr Watson to John Cleese's Sherlock Holmes and between us we devised a fine and simple plan. The 'Clean-up TV' campaign, as it then was, was blazing away nightly at the BBC. The newspapers would print the scores every morning: 'Those who objected strongly to the naked breast that leapt onto our screens last night at 11.43 – 708. Those who rather enjoyed it – 0.' This of course is easily arranged. As Mrs W herself says:

'But I also know the "average viewer" – and listener – is a good deal less organised than the various pressure groups which are against any form of censorship in this field, especially when it goes against their particular interests. I was very interested to hear, for instance, that by the midday following the BBC's decision not to transmit

the *So You Think You've Got Problems* programme dealing with lesbianism, over 250 objections to the decision had been received by phone! The "Gay Liberation" lobby at work with a vengeance. The response to any radio programme is always very small – and this was at 6.15 on Sunday evening – the kind of people listening then are not normally burned up on the topic of lesbianism. One can only hope the BBC recognised it for the reaction it was!'

I would have thought the reverse was more accurate in that, by and large, those who enjoy naked breasts and the like on television are not going to ring up the Beeb's duty officer and say 'Thank you for the excellent tit in the last programme'. On the other hand, if well-organised campaigners are forewarned that they will be shocked to the foundations of their souls if they tune into a certain programme at a certain hour, and are further instructed on receipt of said shock to phone the Beeb's duty officer and complain bitterly, they are certain to win the night.

What Cleese and I conceived was an equally well-regimented gang of viewers who would strike at a pre-arranged moment and reverse the morning's totals. We could imagine the newspaper reports the next morning: 'The BBC was inundated with phone-calls last night complaining about Jan Leeming's handling of the news. Those who said they had expected her to tear off her clothes and writhe breathlessly on the news-desk singing *See What the Boys in the Backroom Will Have,* and were extremely disappointed that she didn't – 908. Those who expected nothing of the sort – 0.' Another we planned was 'Why was there no foul language during the more pessimistic weather forecasts?'*

In retrospect, we should have done it. It would have perked up the news and weather, if nothing else. As it is, I must set off in the steps of David Attenborough and his *Look at Life* edition 963, Dr Bronowski and his *Ascent of Man* without oxygen, Dr Jonathan Miller's Body and the *Shock of the Nude* and come up with a massive series on the history of sex coupled, if that's the word, with a glossy coffee-table book

(with legs £2.00 extra. VAT not inc.) Or, conversely, this tome. The problem lies in mapping out the route.

Mother Whitehouse in *her* sex book follows man through the Renaissance, dropping names like Michelangelo, Leonardo da Vinci, Galileo, Columbus, Magellan and Drake. She trots briskly through the Ages of Reason and Revolution, man's discovery of 'his uniqueness and the wonders of the world', 'the glory of liberation from superstition', mastery of scientific matter and creative expansion, to Hiroshima where 'original sin, so long denied, manifested itself'. Then comes our sharp decline in the face of man's capacity for evil until in the 1950s the great beast himself arose, Satan incarnate: Sir Hugh Carleton-Greene! ('If anyone were to ask me who, above all, was responsible for the moral collapse which characterised the 1960s and 1970s, I would unhesitatingly name Sir Hugh Carleton-Greene.') He apparently was not alone in opening the floodgates to a tide of filth. The Bishop of Woolwich stands accused with his 'Honest to God', 'dealing a body blow to the Church militant', while 'the BBC late-night satirists, three-times weekly, played merry hell with our institutions, our leaders, our standards, our faith.'

Hang about, Mother W, that's me! Advocating, I gather, throughout the punch-drunk 'sixties, pre-marital sex, abortion on demand, and homosexuality. Plus 'abuse of the monarchy, moral values, law and order and religion'. Who, me? According to Mrs Whitehouse, the activities of the 'liberators' of the 1960s and the psychologists, sociologists, progressives and Gay Liberationists of the 1970s have resulted in the final plummet into the septic tank of the 1980s.

Well, I shall trip along the same route in the prints of her sensible brogues and see if we live on the same planet. Wish me luck as you wave me goodbye.

* *One of my happiest memories is of Jack Scott, doyen of weathermen, emerging late at night from Television Centre having just given the night's last prophecy, whispering 'Shit!' at the pouring rain and dashing back inside for an umbrella.*

IN THE BEGINNING WAS THAT WORD

'What is pornography to one man is the laughter of genius to another' – D. H. Lawrence.

'It is far better to laugh at sex than write *Lady Chatterley's Lover;* a grisly, humourless and largely fatuous diatribe' – M. Muggeridge.

Years ago, in the days of silent television, under the aegis of an infant *Private Eye,* I had my first book published. It was a collection of cartoons, rather brilliantly entitled *William Rushton's Dirty Book,* which is still enjoyed, if a recent correspondent is to be believed, in the universities of Lusaka and Dar-es-Salaam. The great coup was to get Malcolm Muggeridge (this was in 1964, remember, a while prior to his conversion on the Reigate Bypass) to write the introduction. In it he wrote the above re Lady Chatterley, and bemoaned the fact that 'the really terrible thing about the pornography now showered so relentlessly and profusely upon us, is its total seriousness'. 'No one', he added, sage as a brush, 'ever used Rabelais to assist masturbation'. My *Dirty Book,* he said, showing enormous generosity and sweetness of spirit, as I don't think he'd read it at the time, 'delightfully upholds the pious proposition that sex is funny, and presupposes a sense of humour in the Deity which is by no means evident in all His works. A less humorous God would have thought of a different way of reproducing the species. We may be grateful for ours.'

I'm not quite sure, looking back at 1964 from this range, that I thought sex *was* that funny. There was pathetically little about as far as I was concerned. I weighed sixteen-and-a-half stone in those days and, with the Fatty Arbuckle case still fresh-ish in female minds, my jokes about sex were delivered in much the same spirit as those of your perky Cockney during the Blitz. They invariably involved fat couples eager to be at it, dancing nakedly about one another but humorously doomed. The story of my life? I can see the question poised like Esther Williams on the springboard of your lip. You'll never know. There are too many dead grey cells. This is why a) you'll never get an autobiography out of me, and b) I cannot support the BMA's attitude to brain death. I'm certain they could find empty pockets of grey cells lurking round the back of my skull that would convince them that I was no more, despite the fact that round at the front I was conversing cheerfully on any number of subjects.

I envy Clive James his total recall of long-distance, two-fisted ejaculating under a southern sun. Well, perhaps not that much envy. I can remember, some time round the summer of 1942, competing in an altitude urinating contest in a small, roofless brick *pissoir* by Jew's Wood on the road to Risca, which was in Monmouthshire when last I saw it. I couldn't even clear the porcelain but there were lads who could clear the brickwork. Great arcs of piddle flashed against the sun like an inter-galactic dog-fight. People at the bus-stop rushed for the shelter of the wood. And there was a war on. I envied my contemporaries their prowess as I envy C. James his memory. Then again *he* envied the long-distance wanker. Take heart, Clive baby, people who can piss over walls never get to write about it – they become solicitors and chiropodists.

How is it that I remember bits of 1942, yet very little of 1964? How can I remember when I first learnt the facts of life? I was at a strangely cosmopolitan preparatory school which had its own Captain Grimes who was perfect in every

detail, down to the wooden leg. The head boy was a Turk, and the first three in the batting-order were Chinese, sons of diplomats. Thus, when Chiang Kai-Shek retreated to Formosa, they left and we never won another game despite a formidable pair of opening bowlers, both Persian.

I caught measles or mumps or chicken pox at the end of a term and found myself sharing the sick-room in an empty school with, I think, Jones III: not Chinese at all, and a knowing boy, a year or so older than myself. He revealed all. I remember thinking how it all seemed quite possible, but not for a second could I picture my parents at it. I wasn't shocked, but it seemed impossible. I could imagine any other duet in the world engaged in Mother Nature's tacky dance – Matron and Mr Leyland, the French master; the Chief Scout and Dr Edith Summerskill; even Flanagan and Allen, but not . . . Good Lord! or Yaroo! or Cripes! or whatever we said out loud in those days, not *them!* I proposed an alternative which impressed Jones III enormously: the use of a hypodermic.

But for a few details which I would have left to others anyway, I invented artificial insemination at the age of ten or so. I should have stayed with it really. I might now be chairman of some vast international chain of sperm banks. 'If we could bottle Pope John-Paul II, gentlemen, what a seller!' (And what a service; he does seem the sort of person who ought to be propagated.) I was therefore convinced that I was the happy result of a series of jabs, but was determined to check this out at source. I could have phrased the question better, however. When the mumps had subsided or the spots vanished, my parents came up to Buckinghamshire to fetch me. I was sitting in the back of the car and, seizing a pause between Mother's paragraphs, I enquired 'Did you phuck?' (Jones III hadn't given me the correct spelling.) They ossified as one. Magritte might have had an eagle coming through the windscreen of the Ford Popular, but otherwise they were posing perfectly for him. Father coughed and laughed, Mother accelerated and began to speak of other things equally speedily. Answer came there none.

From then on I worked on hearsay and maps of the backs of rabbits. And the soft porn of the late 1940s such as the serialisation of *Forever Amber* in the *Sunday Dispatch.* A racy moment I discovered in *Cakes and Ale.* I could hardly wait to be old enough to unlace a bodice. Then I was introduced to Mickey Spillane, and discovered that there were women who didn't wear bodices. The blood began to pump a little faster and there were faint stirrings in the grey flannel. Was I depraved? Was I corrupted? Not at all. It certainly seemed a lot more fun than a course of injections.

Another surprise, not shock, was to discover the word 'fuck' in print. It doesn't look at all as it

sounds, though this is probably true of all words, particularly if you can't read. But it's quite a shapely word. You can walk around it and it's not unattractive from any angle. I first met it in print during a surreptitious thumb through a paperback edition of *Lady Chatterley* Father had smuggled in from France in Mother's smalls before the war.

Round about edition 20 of *Private Eye* we thought of printing that word on the cover. There would be a beautifully illuminated 'F' and 'U' and 'C' and 'K' mounted on each corner of the page, below which would appear the tasteful legend 'This word *can* be beautiful'. For some reason we didn't and indeed, come issue 500 in February 1981 when I drew the commemorative cover, that word was again removed within five minutes of entering the office.

Suffice to say that I was a lad entering the 1950s, knowing precisely what one of these fucks was and how to spell it. As the late great Kenneth Tynan said in 1966 on *Not So Much a Programme* (a thrice-weekly satire programme that caused the end of the world as Mrs Whitehouse knew it): 'I doubt if there are rational people to whom the word "F-f-f-f-f-f-fuck" would be particularly diabolical, revolting or totally forbidden.' His stammer had created the first truly shocking 27-letter word ever heard on television. And, oh, the furore, the fuss and the fol-de-rol! Inspired by this simple statement of fact, which only revealed the appalling lack of rational people, I was moved to write a song of praise to that word for a Bernard Braden show that was running at the time. The song contains an appalling error, however. That word is not Anglo-Saxon at all. It came to us via Scotland* from a German word 'ficken' which means to pound in a mortar with a pestle.

Anyway, a quick burst of song, and then back to the beginning of it all and a study of the Deity's sense of humour.

* *Via Burns, in fact, according to the* Classical Dictionary of the Vulgar Tongue. *It occurs in Florio's definition of* fottere – *'To jape; to saide, to fucke; to swive, to occupy'. From the Greek* phuteo, *Latin* futuere, *the French* 'foutre'. *The medial 'c', it says, comes from a Teutonic root.*

SONG (IN 'F')

What is it that Britain has created,
Of which all foreigners most jealous be?
What assails your ears
In both the hemispheres
And is said and done by them, and you and
    me?

That word! That word! That old four-letter
    word!
It stands for something beautiful,
It's to the point, and brief,
It doesn't take too long to say it
And it brings intense relief!

That word! That word! That Anglo-Saxon
    word!
From Khartoum to the Khyber Pass.
'Gainst Dervishes and Boers,
It's stood by Tommy through the years;
It's won a dozen wars.

Yet some cry out on hearing it
'Let he who said that, rue it!
We don't say that in front of our wives!'
We doubt if they even do it.

That word! That word! That old four-letter
    word!
When faced with life's calamities
What would we do without it?
Obscene, perhaps, but British!
No wonder that we shout it!
That word! That word!
That wonderful one-two-three-four-letter
    word!

THE ORIGINAL SIN

The Holy Ghost had been getting on God's wick for a good forty days and forty nights, shaking his head and saying 'Now what?' and 'Follow that!'

'Have I not', asked God, most reasonably, 'made the heavens and the earth, and all the host of them? And come up with Man, a living soul, and given him the nostril of life? And planted a garden eastward in Eden and put him in it? What more do you want?'

'Well', said the Holy Ghost, 'are you just going to leave him there on his tod, or what?'

'He has the garden to look after.'

'I was thinking more of a bit of company for him', said the Holy Ghost.

And the LORD God said, 'It is not good that the man should be alone; I will make an help meet for him.'

'Now you're talking', said HG.

And out of the ground the LORD God formed every beast of the field, and every fowl of the air; and brought them unto Adam to see what he would call them.

'That should keep him occupied', said God.

And while Adam was quite happy pottering around the garden, pointing at birds and saying 'Fish!' and then making a note of it, or shouting 'Okapi!' after a passing herd of bees, the Holy Ghost could see that there was still something missing in his life. God took HG's point, caused a deep sleep to fall upon Adam, took one of his ribs and made a woman. And Adam said, 'This is now bone of my bones, and flesh of my flesh: she shall be called Woman, because she was taken out of Man.' And, given his previous record, her name wasn't too bad – he might well have jotted her down as 'cow' or 'dung-beetle'. Then came the unfortunate business of the serpent and the apple and the sudden fig-leaves and God, who is short-tempered at the best of times but particularly brusque in the Old Testament, cursed them roundly, handed them their coats and ejected them forthwith from the Garden of Eden, putting cherubims on the door to see they didn't wheedle their way back in.

'We have now', said the Holy Ghost, 'reached the end of Genesis Chapter 3, and I am bound to reiterate "Now what?"'

'That's up to them', said God.

'What I mean is', continued the Holy Ghost, 'the rib business is none too efficient. Anyone eager for a large family will cave in after a time. To be fair, they're not going to come up with the notion of sex off their own bats, are they?'

God was idly wondering why dinner was

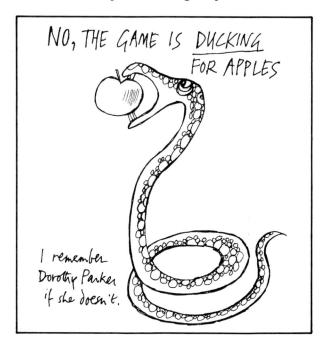

NO, THE GAME IS DUCKING FOR APPLES

I remember Dorothy Parker if she doesn't.

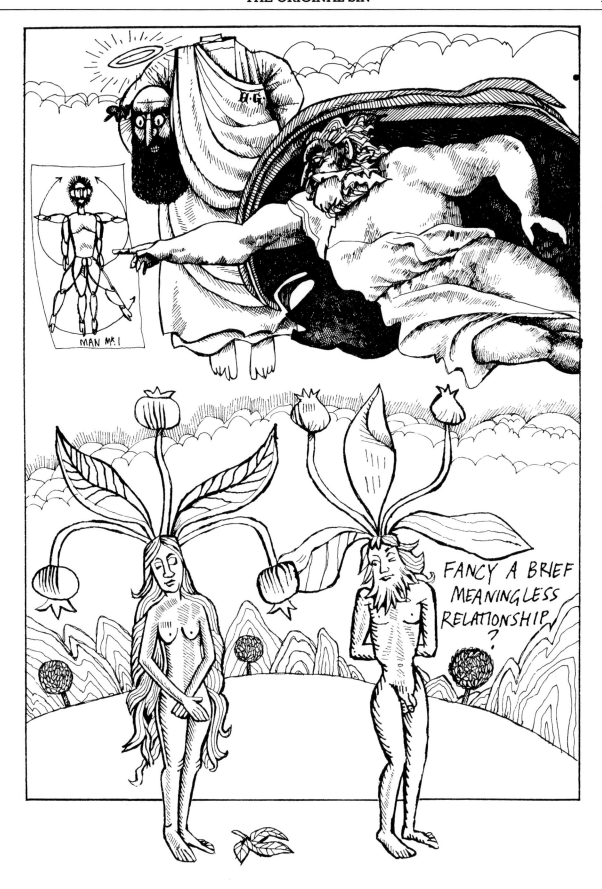

late, and then realised that he hadn't created it yet.

'We could drop pamphlets and instruction manuals', HG persisted. 'Otherwise it's going to be very hard for them to put two and two together.' He then roared with laughter at what he thought might, in the fullness of time, be a joke.

'A gong would be good', pronounced the Almighty. 'And puddings.'

'Blimey!' said the Holy Ghost, marvelling at His inventiveness. 'And I thought you were going to split the Adam!' Once again, he rolled with laughter.

'If', said God, 'we propagate this particular species, we must devise a system that is fail-safe'.

'You mean', said HG, 'a system whereby nothing would happen if members of the opposite sex should bump into each other accidentally in the wilderness, or explore each other's ears with a finger? Clapping their eating-holes together can be pleasurable, but useless?'

'Quite so', said God.

'Well, what have we got?' asked HG. 'You made Adam in your image.'

'Slightly more compact', said God. 'Not so large: there's not enough room. It's a small world.'

'But a very large universe', HG pointed out.

'I could hardly be expected to get it all right first time', said God peevishly. 'I had quite a few stabs at Earth, and left them up as they're very pretty, a cause for wonderment, and provide the lighting.'

'If you ask me', said HG, pointing at the blueprints on the wall, 'it looks like *that* bit and *that* bit'. And at this, they both roared with uncontrollable mirth.

And Adam knew Eve his wife; and she conceived (*Genesis Chapter 4 verse 1*), which in the circumstances was fairly remakable: Adam was 930 years old when he died.

Biblical Beauties

The Magazine for Playboys of the Middle Eastern World

GETTING STONED
Interview with a very fortunate Adultress.

THE SCARLET WOMEN OF GATH · A Probe

THE SODOM I KNEW · LOT TALKS!

BORING CONFESSIONS OF A EUNUCH

The exotic Jezebel seen here looking for a good time.

OUR COVER GIRL!

Drinking to Beget p.27

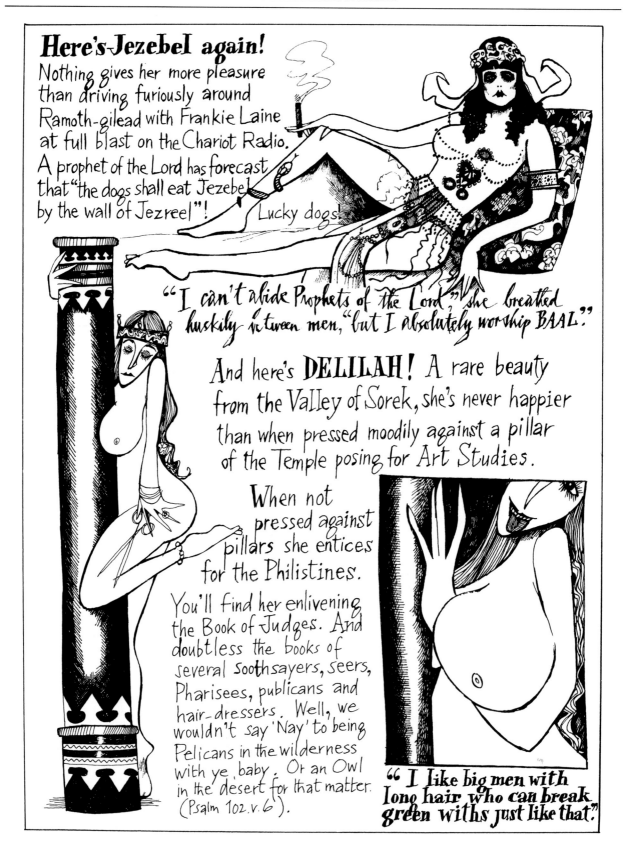

Here's Jezebel again!

Nothing gives her more pleasure than driving furiously around Ramoth-gilead with Frankie Laine at full blast on the Chariot Radio. A prophet of the Lord has forecast that "the dogs shall eat Jezebel by the wall of Jezreel"!   Lucky dogs!

"I can't abide Prophets of the Lord," she breathed huskily between men, "but I absolutely worship BAAL."

And here's **DELILAH!** A rare beauty from the Valley of Sorek, she's never happier than when pressed moodily against a pillar of the Temple posing for Art Studies.

When not pressed against pillars she entices for the Philistines.

You'll find her enlivening the Book of Judges. And doubtless the books of several soothsayers, seers, Pharisees, publicans and hair-dressers. Well, we wouldn't say 'Nay' to being Pelicans in the wilderness with ye, baby. Or an Owl in the desert for that matter. (Psalm 102. v. 6).

"I like big men with long hair who can break green withs just like that."

Not all the Action's in the Old Testament!

Whisper it not in Gath, or indeed Electrithity but Salome has never had a Dancing Lesson in her Life! "I am not ashamed of my lovely breasts" she moues, "They should not be hidden under a bushel."

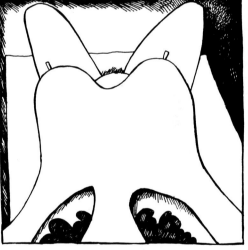

" I enjoy torrid affairs with Men of Letters — it began when I leaped from a Giant Begel at a Literary Breakfast in Caesarea."

WHEN THEY BEGAN TO BEGET

Having mastered the basic principles, the early Biblicans then began to beget like rabbits. They begat all over the place. The fact that they were all closely related during those early begattings could explain why God, in his infinite wisdom, decided to drown the lot like a bag of cats. Only Noah appears to have begat with a cousin distant enough to satisfy the Almighty and, despite his advanced years (he was over 600), was advised to take to the Ark.

When the waters finally receded and the entire population of the planet Earth – Noah and his wife, Shem and Mrs Shem, Ham and Mrs Ham and Mr and Mrs Japheth – were stretching their legs on the top of Mount Ararat, God appeared with what must have seemed a pretty tall order. 'Be fruitful', He said, 'and multiply; and replenish the earth'. Old Noah was obviously excused fruitfulness and multiplying, but the lads set to with a will, all the way through Genesis Chapters 10 and 11. Indeed, such a vast family group was established that, when a tower-block was built to house them all at Babel, God was obliged to introduce severe linguistic differences between them, in order that they'd be encouraged to travel. This policy appears to have backfired over the years, but it was the only way to separate them at the time, except for an enormous bucket of cold water.

Abraham had an interestingly modern relationship that would have given Mrs W cause to pause. His wife, Sarah, could not begat to save her life, and she suggested to Abraham – and this could well be viewed as 'progressive' behaviour – that he should have it away with Hagar, their Egyptian *au pair.* This led ultimately to a bit of domestic strife, but a child was born who seems to have been some-

thing of a china egg, for some sixty years later Sarah gave birth to Isaac.

Throw in murder, violence, war, a population explosion and the smutty goings-on that caused the Lord to wipe out Sodom and Gomorrah with fire and brimstone and it would appear that, by about a third of the way through Genesis, mankind had established a pattern of behaviour it hasn't got over yet. What went on precisely in *Gomorrah* is a bit difficult to pinpoint. One gathers that 'the men of Sodom were wicked and sinners before the LORD exceedingly' and one can just imagine the sort of thing they were up to, perhaps as a reaction against the unrelenting multiplying and begatting, but pretty unacceptable nevertheless; but on another occasion the Lord complained to Abraham about both Sodom *and* Gomorrah 'because their sin is very grievous'. Not very helpful; and if anyone knows of someone who has been gomorrahed, answers on a postcard please.

Q	What causes a population explosion?
A	An enormous number of small bangs.

Before leaving the Old Testament, which should be taken with a pillar of salt anyway, here's a cautionary tale from Chapter 38. If one learns anything from the Old Testament it is this: nothing can stop the rot, despite the constant presence of the ultimate do-gooder Himself personally cajoling, threatening and smiting, His behaviour fluctuating between the White-houseian and the positively Thatcheresque. (Can it be that the moral, social and economic welfare of our great nation lies in the hands of

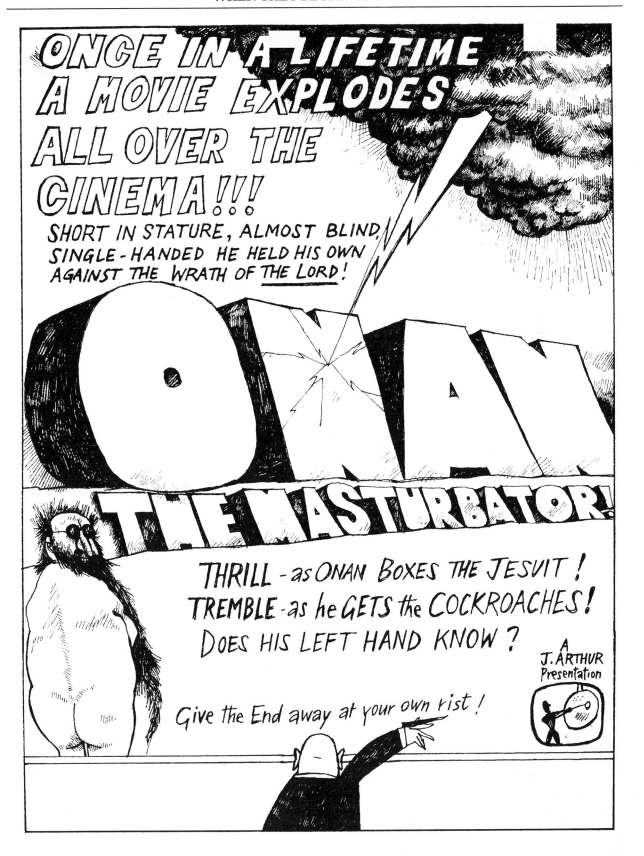

two batty women from the Midlands?) It's no small wonder He gets mad. Take Chapter 38, and his really appalling treatment of a man who has given his name to an act of solitary pleasure that never hurt a fly. (That may be too large a claim; the odd fly may have been damaged over the years, but that is a matter that lies between entomologists and their consciences.)

'Judah went down from his brethren', apparently, 'and turned into a certain Adullamite, whose name was Hirah'. I thought that was quite racy, but an Adullamite appears to be a lay-by, because 'Judah saw there a daughter of a certain Canaanite, whose name was Shuah; and he took her, and went in unto her'. Just like that, and probably without removing his socks. I imagine the telephone-lines are blocked solid with laments about that sort of thing. Inevitably, in the foulness of time 'she conceived, and bore a son; and he called his name Er'. Probably in honour of the certain Canaanite. Are you absolutely certain, Canaanite? Er. Er. Now enter our hero. 'She conceived again, and bore a son; and called his name Onan. And she yet again conceived and bore a son and called his name Shelah.' A fine start in life for any lad.

In the very next verse – thus time flies when you're having a good time – 'Judah took a wife for Er his first-born, whose name was Tamar. And Er, Judah's first-born was wicked in the sight of the LORD; and the LORD slew him.' Time also whistles by when you're having a bad time. One has the impression that we are only being blessed with edited highlights.

'And Judah said unto Onan, "Go in unto thy brother's wife, and marry her, and raise up seed to thy brother".' (I'm mildly concerned about the meaning of this, but will press on. Admit it, it's torrid stuff. The duty officer's going potty.) 'And Onan knew that the seed should not be his; and it came to pass' – in a big way it transpires – 'when he went in unto his brother's wife, that he spilt it on the ground, lest he should give seed to his brother.'

> **Interesting aside** *Dorothy Parker had a canary called Onan because it, too, spilt its seed upon the ground. We had a goldfish called Portnoy, for very much the same reason, but not entirely.*

Now comes the crunch. 'And the thing which he did displeased the LORD: wherefore he slew him also.' Now this, in my view, is a pretty heavy over-reaction on the part of the LORD. It is generally accepted nowadays that the very worst that can happen as a result of substantial seed-spilling is a tendency to dwarfishness, short-sightedness, pimples and insanity and even that's a load of poppycock. Apart from which, meeting your Maker in mid-judder must be an appalling experience, particularly when it's your Maker who has just withdrawn you from circulation.

It's such an innocent pastime and yet 'Onanist!' – or word to that effect – is bellowed scornfully from the terraces.* Dictionaries refer to masturbation as 'self-abuse', or 'self-pollution', which is even worse. In the end, it is a leisure activity and free to boot. What more does the Government want – apart from money? Poor Onan; framed, in my view.

Judah, on the other hand, met up with Tamar-the-much-widowed and, thinking she was a harlot, gave her one for the price of a goat. The result was twins and their begatting borders on the unusual. Out popped a little hand, around which the midwife tied a red thread to mark the first-born. The hand withdrew. And out popped the other twin: the original 'After you, Claud!' 'No, after you, Cecil!' Nary a smite. Not a thunderbolt. The LORD kept a very low profile on that one.

*	I was once involved in a deep discussion about football with Malcolm Macdonald.
   'Whatever happened', I enquired, 'to the W-formation?'
   'Arsenal still play it', he replied cheerfully. 'Wankers!'

THE ORIGIN OF THE SPECIOUS

If you're a Darwinian as opposed to a Reaganite, and lean more towards the Theory of Evolution than the OT version, then what were your ancestors up to? They were evolving in ever-increasing circles. While other creatures were making rather more ambitious plans for the future by getting airborne or learning to breathe underwater, Man was tentatively descending from the trees and trying to walk upright. Probably the last time he was really happy was when he was swinging from tree to tree, chomping on a banana and cheerfully mating (not necessarily in that order, or indeed all at the same time). Nevertheless, down he came and slowly and painfully stood up, thus bequeathing his successors bad feet, backache and vertigo. And, unlike the more sensible of God's creatures, he proceeded to take on Mother Nature at every opportunity.

Gone forever was the simple life. Graduating through the Desmond Morris Advance School of Body-language, Homo erectus decided to inject a little sophistication into basic mating, which had hitherto consisted of getting a leg over every spring. Soon it became a series of nudges, winks, grunts and knee-tremblings and – once he'd learnt the art of tree-felling – primitive foreplay, which comprised a seductive rap behind the female ear-hole with a lump of willow and a sharp drag back to the cave. Once again, we are aware of more than a glimmer of the shape of things to come.

Back in the cave Harry Cro-Magnon (for it is he) would, with a series of noises not dissimilar to a Glaswegian going the whole Hogmanay into his cap, attempt to whisper sweet nothings into his recumbent lodestar's shell-like. She, recovering slowly from the passionate mugging, would quite rightly plead a headache (another hangover from those times which is still alive and throbbing today and not, I believe, mentioned in *The Naked Ape*). Harry ups and daubs on the wall of the cave a quick study in clay and bison-droppings of two great hairy mammoths rutting.

'That would look a lot better', she snorts, 'over there. Anyway, it's not straight.'

With his simple stone hammer and flint chisel, he moves 'Two Great Hairy Mammoths Rutting: A Study' to the other side of the cave, laboriously reworks it, sets it straight, stands back and eyes his mate with new dread.

'The legs are all wrong', is all she says and begins to plump up the sabre-tooth-tigerskins viciously. In the absence of the brief expletive (though, unbeknownst to Harry, some Neanderthal krauts are working on one as they pound pterodactyl bones in rude mortars with their early pestles), he roars, 'Two great hairy mammoths rutting!'

'Filth!' she ripostes and, as soon as the last

THIS IS THE FIRST LORD PILLOCK

GUIDE

dinosaur has keeled over from mental exhaustion and it's safe to go out again, he stomps from the cave in search of a primitive urge.

The next mate is no better. He builds her a rather advanced – possibly even the first – hut, by lashing together branches and covering them in turfy sods. She complains bitterly of the problems of dusting grass, the difficulties of decorating the underside of a turfy sod, and the fact that the pictures won't stay up. In addition, despite the advanced nature of the design, it

simply cannot cope with the British climate or falling neighbours. Already, incidentally, we see the weather playing a part in our relationships. Harry thumps her disconsolately over the head with a Brontosaurus thigh-bone and proceeds to mate sadly. It is soon apparent to him that, with an unconscious female under him and water dripping on his back, no good will come of it as far as he is concerned. 'There must be more to life than this', he thinks, forming one of the great original thoughts of the period, on a par

with 'Grunt, I'm bloody hungry' and 'Wau-au-gh! I could give that one a whack with a sand-filled sock'. And he decides to dedicate the rest of his life to getting the square wheel on the road.

Meanwhile, back in the twentieth century, only the prospect of a bad press is preventing some American scientists from firing human sperm up a female chimpanzee. It could be that the synopsis of a lively film lies herein, worth hawking up and down Sunset Boulevard or Wardour Street. *The Bride of Frankenstein out of King Kong,* or vice versa, could be what the moguls are searching for in the smoking ruins of their cigar-butts. But, in the real world, what are those scientists hoping to achieve? In 1967, apparently, the Chinese actually managed to impregnate a chimpanzee by injecting the she-ape with the juice of a small Chinaman. It remained pregnant for three months, but died of cultural revolution shock.

The Yerkes Primate Centre in Georgia has had the capability to perform a similar feat since 1976. 'Not just a wild idea', cries the director. Yes, it is. What will these loonies do with the progeny? What will the progeny do? Will it be stuck in a zoo or will it be sent to Princeton? Will it be allowed to vote? Will they name its father? Perhaps a cocktail of Robert Redford, Henry Kissinger and Norman Mailer will be prepared? Why bother anyway? All they'll come up with is something akin to Harry Cro-Magnon's eldest, and what will that tell us? If the man-ape speaks, what will it have to talk about? Will it ring up the duty officer? Will it become an adviser to President Reagan?

For it was Reagan who, in answer to some presidential campaign query ('Guess The Question' used to be a popular parlour game),

suggested that there might be more to the Old Testament version of creation than met the eye. This could well have been either because he is quite harmlessly deranged or was touting for votes among America's host of religious freaks and freakish religions. Or, tell the truth, both.

It would appear in this case to be the latter. A new sect is apparently pounding up the charts, whose followers firmly believe that we all started exactly as per Genesis Chapter 1 verse 1, and doubtless sell T-shirts, ashtrays, beach-bags, duvet covers, commemorative medallions, glossy coffee-table Old Testaments and the like to spread the word. It's known as Creationism, and they're taking on the evolutionaries in a big way. The director of the Creation Research Centre in San Diego took his kid's school to court, and had the hapless thirteen-year-old in court to testify that he had been told he had 'evolved from apes'. The judge compromised and ruled that henceforth Californian state schools must leave the issue of our origins open. I lean towards a theory I found in a Simon Raven novel that God's brain exploded and we're the unhappy result. We're all bits of totally bewildered grey matter floating about in limbo. If it didn't explode then, you could hardly blame it for doing so now. All this may not seem to have much to do with sex as such, but it establishes that, no matter how the species originated – whether it was the Big Bang or the Rib Job – the propagation principle is the same. The Bard's 'beast with two backs' still roams the verdant pasture, even if God's head aches. We also have proof positive that the world is a vale of weirdos and fruitcakes.

THE GREEKS

I remember sitting in a pub opposite the Mermaid Theatre after a show, enjoying the company of theatrical folk, who represent a very fair cross-section of the four sexes. In five-pint mood, I remember booming, 'Bisexuality would seem to be the answer in a perfect world. Six more pints, Doris, two crème de menthe frappés and a platter of rat-free rissoles!' The general trend of the conversation, as I recall, was that it really should be a source of some regret that one cannot find it in one's heart to fancy one's fellow-man – or woman, if you're a woman – because it seems such a terrible waste of a good half of the human race. It would be a cheering thought that, if you're spurned or feel rejected by the other half, there is still another half with which to pass those giddy moments that restore and invigorate and give cause for cheerful whistling and are, I learnt somewhere, the rough equivalent of a good five-mile hike.

'Alas!' I pontificated loudly, well into my sixth

Judge Peter Solomon commented: "I must consider the resentment and anger of people who go to the cemetery to visit the graves of loved ones, and who may be deterred from doing so by the large number of homosexuals who cavort about there."
He fined Jeffrey £250 with £250 costs.

pint now, 'Fancying my fellow-man has never been my bent, but then neither have liquorice or discotheques.' The general feeling seemed to be that heterosexuality was uncharitable, *chacun à son pouf.* What the hell anyway, nobody's business but yours, goodnight Doris, and away to whatever gets you through the

night and doesn't cause a bout of the cold sweats in the morning.

I was delighted to discover later that, had there been any Ancient Greeks present, they would have heartily applauded our sentiments, probably bought several rounds of drinks, and doubtless regaled us with a number of off-

colour stories about their gods. How lucky they were to have gods whose activities and proclivities make *Dallas* seem like a soggy Sunday evening in central Solihull. There are doubtless some of you out there who can resort to the confessional, but for the rest of us it would certainly help to shift the guilt in mid-peccadillo if one knew that, up there on Mount Olympus or wherever your personal deity squats, there were frolics afoot that would give Hugh Hefner a much-needed inferiority complex.*

Imagine, if you will, the outcry if the Archbishop of Canterbury had to announce from the pulpit that he had received somewhat unnerving reports of God's behaviour, in that He had descended from on high, hijacked a sprauncy treble from the choir-stalls, hoisted him aloft, and was up to the very thing that he in His infinite wisdom had blanket-bombed Sodom for, and in a very big way. And not, the Archbishop would have to admit, as any sort of terrible warning or ecumenical gesture, but for the sheer hell of it. Yet this was precisely the case with Zeus and the charming young cup-bearer, Ganymede. And was there shock, not to mention horror, in Grecian circles? Not a jot. His parents were straight onto the phone to the neighbours, and probably William Hickey, stating their parental pride in young Ganymede: his eight 'O'-levels, his house cricket colours and the fact that he'd been thoroughly abused by Zeus in the guise of the winner of the 4.30 at Thebes.

Not only did your Ancient Greek feel that it was foolish and wasteful to indulge solely in ladies, when indulging in lads as well was twice the fun, but it was legal and above board and if in addition you were jumped on by a minor goddess, hoo-bleeding-ray!

Mrs Whitehouse confesses to not being 'against homosexuals as people', but believes

'homosexual practices to be wrong', and lashes them about the withers with a few verses of Romans 1 to prove it. They have as much right, in her book, 'to be treated with compassionate love as the rest of us'. Very charming of her, very sweet, and up comes her elegant knee, fresh paragraph.

'The *natural* repugnance [the italics are mine, but you're more than welcome: they are included in the price] which most people feel when homosexuality and lesbianism *is* mentioned can result in harshness of attitude and thinking which is, at least, unhelpful and certainly as unchristian as the *perverse practices* which are condemned'.

She maintains vigorously that it is an 'illness', curable by hormones and psychiatry. The medical profession could change the world with hormones. They could certainly change its sex. (*Where The Hormones, There Moan I:* irrelevant old song, but true.) As to psychiatrists, I'm sure they might well have cured the odd homosexual, but then, perhaps the patient wasn't as homosexual as he thought, perhaps he wasn't homosexual at all or perhaps he's still homosexual but, having paid the bill, is desperately trying to prove that he isn't. Thumbing through the newspapers I've noticed that a favourite euphemism for 'homosexualist' is 'married, with two children'.

Incidentally, a fascinating gobbet I culled from the letters to *The Guardian* was that, in the cradle of civilisation, the Edinburgh of the south, the Greek army 'included compulsory homosexuality as part of its training programme'. When I think of the privations I suffered during basic training at Catterick all those years ago in the 5th Royal Inniskilling Dragoon Guards (Irish Cavalry, no less – I was responsible for stuffiing the horses into the tanks. I jest.) The assault course was bad enough, but a sexual assault course would most certainly have spelt the end for 23354249 Trooper Rushton, W. G. The highly-informed letter-writer, Tristan Zeeman (a sitting duck for the crude limerickist, one would have thought) of Liverpool went on to tell us that the Greek colonels of the period felt that the compulsory homosexuality 'induced a heightened sense of comradeship and generally bound the troops closer together'. Mr Zeeman was inspired to

---

* *Here's an example of the kind of behaviour the Greeks could expect. Zeus finally caught his rather reluctant twin sister, Hera, by disguising himself as a mugged cuckoo. When she sought to comfort the battered bird by sheltering it between her breasts, he swiftly turned back into Zeus and Wham! Bam! Thank you, ma'am! The thing about Zeus was that, not only had you no idea which direction he was coming* from, *you had no idea what he was coming as either.*

Homosexuality is now illegal in the British Army after disgraceful scenes in West Germany. Confession is sufficient, no further evidence required. Had that been the case in the 1950s, picture the queues of scented squaddies, hand on hip, waving a limp wrist at the MO.

Rushton: *(in hope of securing discharge) Kiss me goodnight, Sergeant-Major.*

RSM: *Right, on the command 'Kiss' – wait for it! – place the hand firmly to rear of object of desire. Thus,* two, three. *Grasp shoulder-blade seductively between thumb and forefinger of the left hand, two, three. Ascertaining that said object of desire is as straight as the colonel's leg, thrust said object provocatively downwards to an angle of forty-five degrees to the ground, provocativeleeeeee Right, on the command, 'Kiss-Kiss-Kiss'!*

Rushton: *Beg pardon, sir, but our moustaches are inextricably entwined.*

ZEVS RIDES AGAIN - a Cautionary Frieze.

YOU NEVER KNOW WHEN THAT ZEUS WILL POUNCE NEXT. OR WHAT AS. VIZ. I'D KEEP MY EYE ON THAT PLOUGHMAN'S LUNCH ON THE NEXT TABLE. IT'S JUDDERING, AND PLOUGHMAN'S LUNCHES DO NOT, AS A RULE, JUDDER.

AND I'D GIVE THAT PARROT A WIDE BERTH. APART FROM FOUL-PEST, FRIEND ZEUS IS DEEPLY INTO SWAN-UPPING. WHO'S A PRETTY BOY, THEN? AND YOU'RE SUDDENLY LAYING AN EGG.

INCIDENTALLY, THAT TORTOISE BEARS WATCHING. EITHER IT'S GOT A BAD BACK OR ITS PASSIONS ARE HIGHLY AROUSED. YOU NEVER KNOW, DEAR. I NEARLY FELL VICTIM TO A PRAWN COCKTAIL IN THEBES.

NOW HE'S GIVING HIS SCROFULOUS TOM MOGGY. PAY NO ATTENTION TO IT, DEAR, UNLESS YOU KNOW THE WHEREABOUTS OF AN ATHLETIC VET.

PARTICULARLY AS HE'S NOW METAMORPHOSISED INTO A PORKER. IN MY VIEW, ONE OF HIS MORE ACCURATE IMPERSONATIONS.

OH, MY VARIOUS GODS, HE NEVER GIVES UP, DOES HE? DON'T TURN ROUND BUT HE'S NOW COME AS THE WINNER OF THE 3.30 AT DELPHI.

FOR FUTURE REFERENCE, DEAR, KEEP A WARY EYE OUT FOR FISH IN THE BATH AND SNAKES IN THE GRASS. HE GOT HIS MUM LIKE THAT. SNAKED UP HER UNAWARES.

SCREAM! SCREAM! SNAKE! UP! A-A-A-A-AH!

I WOULDN'T TAKE THAT LYING DOWN

pass on this information on reading an SAS advertisement seeking recruits. I think he was probably trying to help, but I get the uneasy sensation every time I mention the SAS in jocular vein that their massed bands will erupt through the windows one night and kick the shit out of the '1812' all over the living-room.

But I digress. No nation, in fairness, can keep up such behaviour forever, and the Greeks slowly began to clean up their act. Zeus had begun to get a particularly bad press and stood accused of quite unnecessarily brutish behaviour. Part of his problem could have stemmed from the fact that he was breast-fed by a sow. (I rang up a psychiatrist on this one, but he refused to comment.) Whether or not he felt this gave him sufficient licence to roger Mother, he did. She, poor Rhea, detecting sinister bulging beneath his vestment, turned rather smartly into a serpent which should have been sufficient to dampen most ardour, snakefetishists being somewhat few and far between. Whereas you or I would have thought twice at this juncture, and indeed probably a good deal earlier, not so Zeus, who also turned himself sharply into a serpent.

Q Could this be the origin of the phrase 'the one-eyed trouser-snake'?

A No. (Actually, it was Barry Humphreys who coined it, *circa* 1963.)

He then wound himself about Mother, totally incapacitating her by means of a full nelson with added cross-buttock, and that was that. Apart from which, and one really is only chipping away at the periphery of his unseemly behaviour, he got Metis, a saucy Titaness, in the club and, on hearing that the unborn child would be a considerable security risk, he swallowed her. He then became the victim, quite rightly you may think, of appalling migraines. One day by Lake Triton, he was struck down with one of these headaches and Hermes, after a quick diagnosis, cried 'Aspirin is not enough!', fetched a hammer and chisel, trepanned him vigorously and out leapt Athene, fully clothed and shouting.

The Greeks began to look for better things from their gods. Eros is a case in point: one might imagine that his popularity would have known no bounds but, in fact, quite the reverse is true. Whereas we think of him as a cheerful little God of Love, occasionally loosing off darts at tarts up Shaftesbury Avenue, your Greek viewed him as a God of Sexual Passion (he never, incidentally, made the top twelve) and was regarded by them as something of a menace. 'Uncontrolled sexual passion', says Robert Graves about the little fellow, 'could be disturbing to ordered society'. Please excuse the shakiness of the handwriting. Perhaps it's equally true that 'controlled' sexual passion isn't exactly healthy either, but the Greeks were slowly getting religion and . . . exit left the glory that was Greece, and package tours today are not what they used to be.

Consenting possibly, Adult certainly, but, gentlemen, I would query the privacy of Parliament Square.

THE ROMANS

Two things leap to mind when faced with the sexual behaviour of the Romans: orgies and the National Theatre. My knowledge of the former is limited, I'm afraid, to Hollywood's notion of Rome in the epics of the 1950s. These consisted of Victor Mature having grapes stuffed down his upturned mouth by a plastic girl, with freckles and bulky brassière, who clearly started her career on the cutting-room floor. Meanwhile, plump cheer-leaders in diaphanous mauve would caper, like a display of geriatrics from the Cardiff Baths, round huge Nubians coated in lard who longed for the days when they packed down for the Los Angeles Rams. There was usually some sort of belly-dance which was about as erotic as a hatful of offal. You somehow expected concubines to enter in red blazers, shouting 'Hail, campers!'

This Hollywood version of the Roman at play may have been the reason that orgies have definitely gone down-market. In the grand old days, one would arrive in the brougham at some great stately, mount the great staircase, hand to the footman with a flourish one's top hat, silver-knobbed cane, cloak, trousers, starch-stiffened dickie, socks and shoes and proceed to the great ballroom for communal romping and flesh-thwacking. Today, advertisements like 'Fun-loving duo, well-preserved, into rubber and left luggage, seek like, South London, alternate Thursdays' seem to attract ill-assorted pairs who park their Ford Cortinas outside Penge villas, furtively dive inside with their canvas hold-alls, toss their car-keys onto the carpet and pray the *News of the World* isn't lurking in the shrubbery. (It's the other woman I'm sorry for at a wife-swapping soirée with the Carlo Pontis.) Apart from providing copy for the *News of the World,* do these people do any harm? If they do, then I suppose it's only to each other. What's more, they probably don't frighten as many horses as the Sunday paper that boasts 'All human life is here'.

There is the happy tale of a probing *News of the World* reporter who was despatched to reveal the all about two prostitutes who used to work in harness as a mother and daughter act. The daughter was clad in full St Trinian's gear which is a turn-on, one gathers, in certain circles. The cub reporter's story went that he had bearded the shameless pair in their lair, studied their wares, leafed through the prospectus, made an excuse and left. 'Made an excuse and left, did he?' screamed the furious 'mother', her bosom heaving with heavy irony, to another Grub Street hack who had turned up, possibly with the intention of eliciting her kiss-and-tell memoirs. She went to the fridge and returned with a rubber device, knotted at the top, labelled with name and date, and clearly used. Waving the evidence, she pointed out that the crusading reporter had made an excuse and come.

The *News of the World,* incidentally, does not feature in Mrs W's extensive 'blue list'. In fact, no newspaper does, which is odd. I imagine most people's introduction to soft porn was through the tatty columns of certain Sundays and, nowadays, the odd daily. From the serialisation of *Forever Amber,* through the endless court proceedings – scoutmasters scouting for boys; parsons de-frocking their flocks; the memoirs of duke's ex-gillies; and Tories at the bottoms of our guardsmen – to kiss-and-tellings of models who've never seen daylight. There's been a wide range of photographs, from the first bikini girls to those

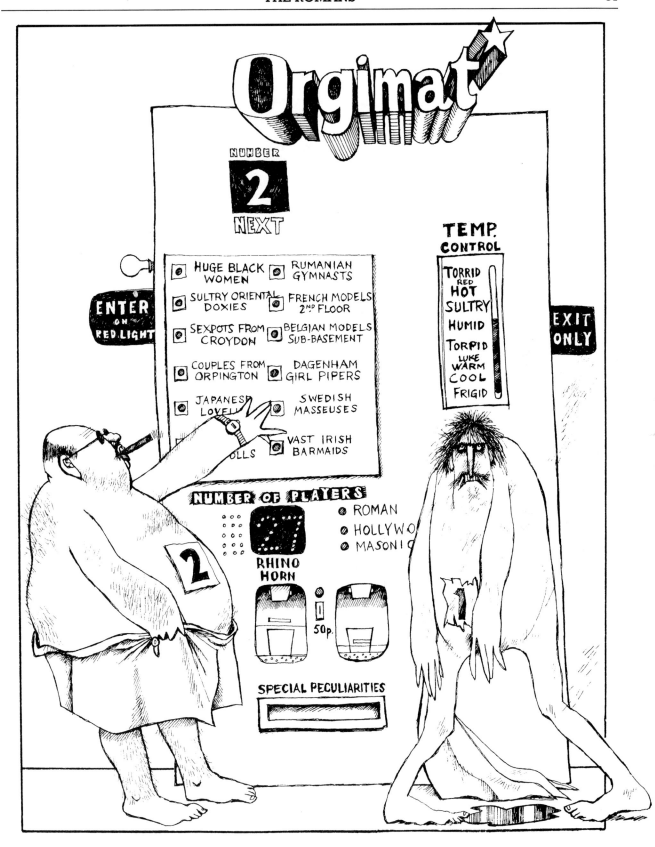

newpapers who can think of nothing more newsworthy to put on their third page than a photograph of yet another woman you've never heard of with no clothes on. There are occasions when I believe the public has a right *not* to know. It is passing strange that Mrs W seems unmoved by tit-in-the-door journalism. If one was totally cynical, one might be excused for thinking it was something to do with good PR. I also have the feeling that 'moral decline' means that orgies are now available to all and are no longer the privilege of Victor Maturus and the nude man in the masonic apron. Whatever happened to the nude man in the masonic apron? Now there's a question.

THE ROMANS IN BRITAIN

I would like here to pay tribute to their major legacy: the fact that they looked at our primitive isle, alive with bogs and rising damp, trod our muddy sheep-tracks, squelched through our living-rooms and decided overall to do something about the flooring. But for their efforts in tiling, flooring and road-laying, we would still be striding through life up to our knees in it. While paying tribute to the Romans in this way, I must concede that it has nothing to do with sex. Very well, there might be more sex on the floor if it were yielding earth, but there would be a deal of women wasted through drowning in the rainy season, or summer as we know it.

The Romans in Britain to whom I refer, however, are the rude legionaries who nightly – and twice on Saturdays – buggered the locals at the National Theatre. Mrs Whitehouse, who hasn't seen the play, has at the time of writing dragged the director, Mr Bogdanov, before the beak under the 1956 Sexual Offences Act. He stands accused of procuring 'the commission by a man of an act of gross indecency with another man'. I haven't seen the play either, and thus feel fully qualified to take issue with her.

Funnily enough, the first person to rise as a man and storm from the auditorium howling 'Disgrace! Disgrace!' was Sir Horace Cutler (the then Führer of the GLC). His comments were massively publicised by the media – for these are easy days in which to create an outcry – but the main reaction to his criticism was a sharp increase in bookings, and queues round the block. This might be deemed a perfectly natural reaction for, if Sir Horace were the health warning on a packet of cigarettes, he would convince most right-thinking people that a packet of twenty contained the fountain of youth, cured the common cold and put lead in your pencil or on your roof of wheresoever you would most enjoy having your lead.

Incensed with indignation Sir Horace stood and, like a comet, burned. Vengeance was his and, with the able support of the chairman of the GLC Arts Committee, who found the play 'the most revolting display I have seen in my life' (clearly a sheltered one), they hit the National in the grant. (One of my few impersonations, apart from sheep being thrown out of a biplane, is an Arts Council grunt.)

All this set Mrs W's dervishes whirling and caused her to wail like a banshee. Not, as I say, having seen the piece, and rather than accept the gospel according to St Horace, I turn for my text to the words of Bernard Levin, late of *The Times,* a man of rare good sense. (Well, one can't exhibit good sense all the time.) He found *The Romans in Britain* to be 'a very good play indeed'. It is written, apparently, in the language of the universal squaddie and, as Mr Levin says of Howard Brenton, the author, he had no great hopes 'that he would have abandoned his extraordinary conviction that "fuck" is another word for "comma" (nor has he, incidentally)'. The play hops ('with very considerable dramatic skill' – B. Levin) between Caesar's invasion of Ancient Britain and Ulster today. Apart from the language as mentioned, it's the buggery bit that has caused all the wailing and the whirling. I quote the learned St Bernard (may hard-boiled quail eggs shower endlessly upon his noble head – I think that is his idea of total bliss):

To my mind, the cheering aspect of the whole laughable business is that, since this play was first performed, I have seen no sign – and I have searched the presses daily for such news – of it having depraved or corrupted. One might well imagine that Druids would be walking our streets in terror of their lives: sidling along, backs to the wall, waving their sickles vigorously at the first signs of trouble, viz a charabanc-load of Italian war veterans. Not at all so. Even at the national Eisteddfod where they were, after all, gathered *en masse* in their easily recognisable robings, there was no report of rapine behaviour. The day a Druid is buggered under the mistletoe, or anywhere else for that matter, and the guilty party admits 'It was the National Theatre that made me do it', I shall send to Mrs Whitehouse a very seemly and apologetic note, with a copy to Sir Horace Cutler. Otherwise, duckies, forget it.

En passant

I was idly glancing through the 'For Sale' columns of *The Guardian* when I came upon a large small-ad for contraceptive devices. The paper seems to carry quite a few of these, but there's nothing wrong with that. It can only be a deal simpler through the post (credit cards accepted), and I've yet to meet a chemist who gives free samples. This advertisement promised '36 Durex Fetherlite, £5.70; 30 Stimula Ribbed, £4.99', and then what I took to read '24 Milton Shaped, £2'. What a tribute, I thought, to one of our greatest poets. Can one get a packet of Byron Shaped, a Box of Betjeman? On studying the ad more closely, I saw that it actually read '24 Million Shaped, £2'. This seems tremendous value and should get even Georges Simenon through a dirty weekend.

I continued my perusal of the column. '20 Strawberry Condoms, £4.50; 12 Hata Stimulating, £2.25; 9 French Ticklers*, £5.60.' I must admit I was entranced; they all seemed such fun. It was like thumbing through a gardening catalogue without the green fingers.

Then I read '18 Roman Way'. A tickler for Latins? An aid to lousy lovers, perhaps? Surely Caligula never bothered? It came as something of a dampener on an otherwise fascinating read to discover that it was their address.

* *Not to be confused with the French Trickler which is, of course, their national flag. If you wish to confuse it with le Trickler,* eh bien, chacun à son goût, *run it up the flagpole and see if anyone salutes it.*

THE DARK AGES

Near St Buryan in Cornwall you'll find a circle of nineteen stones known as the Merry Maidens. Outside the circle are two menhirs. These, legend has it, were two musicians to whose pipings nineteen merry maidens had danced one Sabbath. According to the early Christian Church, the Devil appeared among them and promptly turned them all into stone. This would seem to be blatant propaganda. One's immediate reaction is that the Devil surely would have thoroughly approved of nineteen maidens dancing merrily on a Sunday; he would appear otherwise to be an extremely unlikely founder of the Lord's Day Observance Society. This is pretty typical of the period, however, when the Church took on the old beliefs. Simple souls, who had hitherto found total satisfaction in fertility rites and carving rude graffiti on the chalk Downs of Southern England, now found themselves facing eternal damnation and God knows what for abandoned frolicking round the maypole.

There's a good deal to be said for celebrating the arrival of spring with a bit of a whoopee. Christmas is well-placed for cheering up the middle of winter, but I've never celebrated the New Year with much enthusiasm. There's always something acutely depressing about the Scots Hogmanaying like mad, and I never could stand the strains of *Auld Lang Syne.* Should old acquaintance be forgot? Forget it. It should be noted that 31 December is man-made and no different to 1 January.

Spring is another matter altogether, though. Spring is the time for resolutions. Great powers, you've lasted out another winter, buds are budding, the sap is rising, the days are lengthening and the drawers cellular seem suddenly a size too small. Come, kick off winter's traces, tear off your clothes, your cardigans, your thermals, your clouts, and trip with me upon the verdure; let us dance naked in the springtime sleet. Or, conversely, come up on the Downs and gouge out of the chalk a dirty-old-man-of-somewhere with an enormous thing that can be seen from miles away. And rustic maids will come and clod-hop round it with daisies in their hair and huge breasts jostling like a crowd of Buddhists. And then, just as the party's hotting up and the jolly red-faced girls are squeaking 'This is really *pagan,* Doris!' and 'Primordial's the word, Ethelfilth!', into view hoves a team of sky-pilots chanting something Gregorian, and pointing the finger in no uncertain manner.

Faced with a totally new notion of right and wrong, it was no wonder our forebears were confused. They were used to magic and herbal cures, they probably had the answer to the common cold, they worshipped the sun when it warmed them, and when it poured with rain they reckoned the gods were thoroughly irked and promptly sacrificed the cat. Their clocks were set by the seasons, which beats digital alarms into a cocked hat. Of course, life was fairly brutish, but then last Thursday wasn't exactly a bowl of cherries either.

It comes as no surprise, therefore, that people turned to Old Nick when the Pagans clashed head-on with the Church. What had previously seemed a perfectly reasonable Saturday night out on the Henge, for instance, became the work of the Devil, punishable by an eternity of hell-fire and purgatory as advertised on crude woodcuts. Their reaction was typical of mankind throughout the ages. Observe the effect upon your fellow human driving a yellow Ford Cortina or a juggernaut up a fog-thick, drizzle-

The Dirty Old Man of Basildon.

laden, wind-swept motorway when the lights come up suggesting a more sensible pace of, say, 50 mph. It's like a red rag to a bull. That is the moment to get into the slow lane and pretend you have a limp. Madness it may be, but it's man's natural reaction to being told what to do – and separates him from Barbara Woodhouse's mutts.

Thus was it then, and proof positive that if you stomp about over-vigorously on the good old ways, with ducking-stools and bonfires, putting the fear of God up people in a big way, you end up centuries later – to the delight, admittedly, of the beastlier Sunday papers – with local covens of bank managers and hairdressers meeting on alternate Thursdays in the snug bar prior to practising black masses and dark satanic rites behind the industrial estate at the witching hour.

It boils down to the fact that all those seized by moral or religious fervour and zeal should think, not in terms of black and white, but of ways to brighten the grey.

Interestingly enough, Mrs Whitehouse quotes on her title page the eminently sensible and romantic G. K. Chesterton, who would surely have found her a crashing bore. 'All healthy men, ancient and modern, Eastern and Western, know that there is a certain fury in sex that we cannot afford to inflame, and that a certain mystery and awe must ever surround it if we are to remain sane.'

Lope through the *Dictionary of Quotations* and you will find that he also vouchsafed: 'The men who really believe in themselves are all in lunatic asylums'; 'Bigotry may be roughly defined as the anger of men who have no opinions'; and 'When some English moralists write about the importance of having character, they appear to mean only the importance of having a dull character.'

Let me add that we in the centre are all for mystery and awe, and are sane as hatters.

Fig. 114. DISRESPECTFUL CONDUCT OF THE DEVIL TO A FRIVOLOUS WOMAN

NOT MY BEST SIDE

THE VIKINGS

The Vikings are best remembered, whatever Magnus Magnusson may say, for their pillage and, above all, their rape. Rape, of course, has infinitely more to do with violence than sex, and really cannot be any more gratifying to the perpetrator than assaulting a telephone-box. Sex has to be a friendly business. It's not there solely to boost the numbers of the human race, but is also designed for mutual delight, comfort and reassurance in a beastly world. Surely the Vikings must have realised that it's a pretty mundane business without the whoops of pleasure and cries of 'Wow!' that are the target and ambition of the majority of couplets.

'My word, that was terrific.'
'Did you, my dove, hear bells ringing?'
'That was the best, my chuck, could you move your leg?'
'Was I really all right?'
'More than that. And I?'
'First-rate. Blimey, it beats skittles!'
'May I include you in my next novel?'
'Modesty forbids.'
'Under an assumed name?'
'Righty ho, then.'

All this was lost to the Viking. Indeed, insofar as a sharp knee in the parts, a blast of mace gas from an aerosol, shrill cries of 'Get off, you sod!' and an overall lack of enthusiasm and whooping would put most of us off our length and reduce our manhood to an elfin effigy of the Michelin Man, it's hard to see how much joy can be achieved. No joy is, of course. Why do it then? You can't blame the times we live in: that's the usual trick of those who can't provide an answer to problems that have existed for a thousand years or more. The Vikings, after all, did not have dark blue movies: they had over-active

appetites and bags of swagger. The blame can be laid at the unsavoury feet of what one might today refer to as 'plastic macho' – the male chauvinist's eternal urge to be butch as old boots, which undoubtedly springs from an unnatural fear of women, starting probably with Mother. If it's any comfort, the latest buzz from the slammer is that our most notorious rapist, the Cambridge one, is now a fully-fledged transvestite – futher proof that God has a sense of humour. The Gadabout Swine are still pounding downhill.

Rape is apparently making a comeback in Denmark, which should cheer those old Vikings as they peer down in their sober moments from Valhallah. Indeed all eyes have been on Denmark since 1969, when all their laws relating to pornography, censorship and all lines to Liberty Hall were repealed. The theory – which seemed reasonable – was that, offered all the filth and smut he wanted, the average Dane would yawn, stretch, and go back to everyday Danish pursuits such as hog-slaughtering, making cheese in Lego or wandering the battlements chatting up father's ghost, and that in next to no time Denmark would be pure as the chauffeur-driven nun.

Unfortunately, as soon as it became generally known that Copenhagen was no longer being wonderful beside the mermaid-stuffed waters of the Baltic, but was hot-bedding it in the clouds on the top of the Porn Mountain, charabanc-loads of pleasure-seekers promptly ascended upon them. A vast, new industry blew up, and your average Dane, great or small, who had yawned and stretched at the soft porn of yore, found himself as embroiled as the tourists. Faced with new hard fast porn and exhibitions of live sex (such as the lady who, according to

Mrs Whitehouse – and would she lie on this one? – 'made a name for herself and a great deal of money appearing with stallions and dogs'), it's no wonder that the Danes made the startling discovery that, while not necessarily taking part themselves in performing dog acts or rude turns with a pantomime horse, they were living in the most permissive society on earth. Statisticians moved among them, criminologists and psychiatrists, anthropologists with theodolites and professors of mental hygiene with seismographs. Pros and cons locked horn-rims and wrestled over the startled Danes. They must have wondered what had hit them.

Naturally, the question trembling on your hot lip is, had they not cast off the bondage (second floor: leatherware, catskin cuffs, stout twine, used racks, scavengers' daughters, scavengers' mothers, straitjackets. . . . Silence! The last thing we want is a drooling reader, shuddering with unrequited passion) of censorship in 1969, would they have fallen down the lift-shaft anyway? What were we British at in '69? (My client apologises, m'lud, for that unintentional slip of the tongue.) In fact, we had just given the Lord Chamberlain the hook. He had finally left the stage. Not before time, too; read on to find out what the Good Lord saved us from.

THE WIT AND WISDOM OF THE LORD CHAMBERLAIN

Throughout the years the Lord Chamberlain has been brandishing his large blue pencil and deciding for us what we may or may not be allowed to see. The following gems are among those passages he considered liable to deprave and corrupt.

1966 You are warned that at no time must the character appear in any costume which consists of less than briefs and an effectively controlling opaque brassière.

1887 Omit the frequent swearing which, it should be understood, is no longer usual in these days in respectable drawing-rooms and in the company of ladies and is calculated to give offence to any intelligent and respectable audience.

1962 Omit from Tennessee Williams' *Night of the Iguana:*

'There was a young gaucho named Bruno
Who said about love, this I do know
Women are fine, and sheep are divine
But iguanas are – *numero uno!'*

1958 Omit the Duchess of Rutland.

Winter in Torquay, first page, omit 'constipating'.

In 1813, despite the fact that we were deeply involved in war with France, the Lord Chamberlain demanded the excision of several songs in *Orange Boven* by one Tom Dibdin, as they were 'too personal against Bonaparte'.

1887 The singing of the words of the hymn had better be omitted in such a piece as this. It is calculated to offend the feelings of a certain portion of a mixed audience, if not considered as profanity. The playing of the organ music will suffice.

1964 Cut 'Hail Mary, full of grace, the Lord is with thee, blessed art thou among women and blessed . . .'

Change from 'do biggies' to 'do a-ah'.

Change from 'Oh, Jesus' to 'Oh, Heaven!'

Cut 'like Ida Mortimore's bum'.

Cut 'Oh, just like my moustache, vertical between her thighs'.

1875 Cut 'Boys will be boys, and youth you cannot fetter.
Girls will be girls, and pray what can be better?'

1968 Omit the married sister of the Madonna.

1966 Cut 'And so you think it is miraculous to feed a crowd of people with two measly sardines and a crust of bread, as Christ did. Christian capitalism has done much better since then.'

1958 In the sentence 'Is it true that there the bulls consort with mares, and rams seek after cows, and the males of the partridges do curious things amongst themselves?', delete all reference to the partridges and replace with 'frogs make love in the human language'.

1958 Cut 'I wonder the Lord Chamberlain permits it'.

1957 For 'Ass upwards', substitute 'cock-eyed'.

For 'rogered', substitute 'did'.

For 'camp', substitute 'weird'.

1958 For 'made a balls of the fly', substitute 'made a botch of the fly'.

For 'I'd like to pee', substitute 'I'd like to relieve myself'.

For 'What about that pee?', substitute 'What about that relieving yourself?'

For 'arses', substitute 'rumps'.

For 'Sing, sing – or show your ring', substitute 'Sing, sing – you lovely thing'.

1875 St George must *not* be made up as Prince Albert.

The Daz Song Omit 'You get all the dirt off the tail of your shirt', substitute 'You get all the dirt off the front of your shirt'.

The mock priest must not wear a crucifix on his snorkel.

Omit 'crap', substitute 'jazz'.

Omit from 'We've just consummated our marriage . . .' to and inclusive of '. . . a steaming hot summer's night'.

Omit from 'In return they are willing . . .' to and inclusive of 'The Duke of Edinburgh is a wow with Greek dishes . . .' and substitute 'Hark ye! Hark ye! The day of judgement is at hand'.

Omit '. . . the perversions of the rubber . . .', substitute '. . . the krempels and blinges of the rubber . . .'.

Omit the chamber pot under the bed.

And some fine specimens emerged when he set to work on Spike Milligan and John Antrobus' *The Bed-sitting Room* in 1963, my theatrical début yet. ('Brilliant, bespectacled' – K. Tynan.)

In fairness, when *Ubu Roi* was revived at the Royal Court, he allowed the following sentence to be reinstated: 'He'll blast you with a honk from his rear.'

THE VIEW FROM BEHIND THE NET CURTAINS

During the Christmas school holidays of 1976, forty Bristolians watched every programme on the three television channels. You might think this was an attempt to get into the Record Book of Guinnesses, or some sponsored activity for charity but, in fact, it was to maintain a blow-by-blow, naughty-word-for-word log of sex, violence and strong language ('bloody or stronger' – Mrs W) on the box. Here are their figures:

These strange statistics beg a number of questions:

1. Do you find 'Mentions of sex activity outside *of* marriage' offensive grammatically?
2. How do you categorise a hoary old chestnut such as 'Do you smoke after intercourse?' 'I've never looked.'?
3. Are such phrases as 'I fancy that barmaid' or 'Charles Atlas was my ideal' or 'The lead singer of the Damp Sleeping-bag makes my knees tremble' mentions of sex activity inside or outside marriage?
4. Is 'Would you come back to my digs for a cup of instant coffee?' an attempt at seduction?

		BBC1	BBC2	ITV
1.	Mentions of sex activity outside of marriage, including jokes on the subject, seductions to intercourse and attempts at seduction	59	63	96
2.	Mentions of sex activity within marriage, including jokes on the subject and shown or assumed sex activity	13	13	4
3.	Unmarried sexual seductions, attempted or achieved (included in 1)	22	28	28
4.	Married sexual activity (included in 2)	2	9	2
5.	Acts of injurious human violence	111	75	149
6.	Further mentions of violence (usually the results of injurious violence)	75	21	78
7.	Blasphemies and swear words	84	46	107

5. Is a sudden rendition of *If You Were the Only Girl in the World* all about sex activity outside of?

6. Were *Timon of Athens* or *The Duchess of Malfi* on that week? (She wouldn't like *'Tis Pity She's A Whore* either.)

7. Did they include news programmes, viz 'five acts of injurious human violence'? *News at Ten* could have used their entire quota in '149 dead in massive pile-up on M1'. The further mention ('usually the result of') could have been the cheering news that the final figure was reduced to 78, a juggernaut-load of horsemeat for the Continent having confused the issue.

8. Is 'Married sexual activity' the stuff of drama? Obviously not, though BBC2 tried hardest.

As to the swear-words, I can remember appearing in such a survey once for saying a couple of 'bloodys' on *Late Night Line-up* and touching on George V's dying words, 'Bognor be buggered'. Incidentally *The Dictionary of Modern Quotations* does not include this, but it does record Sherpa Tensing's cheery 'We've done the bugger' from the top of Everest on Coronation Day. Discuss.

Were the forty Bristolians thoroughly screened at the end of the week for signs of depravity or corruption? By then they should have been red-eyed, steaming-loined, panting and contemplating the Tesco chainsaw massacre.

What makes them so different from the rest of us? Are they quite normal?

But both Mrs Whitehouse and Tolstoy had to restrain the audience during question time. Most delegates wanted confirmation that Britain's moral decline was a result of a conspiracy by communists, h o m o s e x u a l s, Hampstead trendies and Soviet agents. But neither speaker could confirm these fears.

DEATH OF A HERO

In 1929 Richard Aldington wrote a charming note at the beginning of his first novel *Death of a Hero:*

'This novel in print differs in some particulars from the same book in manuscript. To my astonishment, my publishers informed me that certain words, phrases, sentences, and even passages, are at present taboo in England. I have recorded nothing which I have not observed in human life, said nothing I do not believe to be true. I had not the slightest intention of appealing to anyone's salacious instincts; if I had wanted to do that, I should have chosen a theme less seriously tragic. But I am bound to accept the opinion of those who are better acquainted with popular feelings than I am. At my request the publishers are removing what they believe would be con-sidered objectionable, and are placing asterisks to show where omissions have been made. If anything "objectionable" remains, the responsibility is, of course, mine. In my opinion it is better for the book to appear mutilated than for me to say what I don't believe.
En attendant mieux,
R.A.'

It makes Chatto and indeed his friend Windus, the publishers, look quite silly, and rightly. It also lends enormous mystery to the book. I quote:

'"Time passes", said George; "what do we know of Time? Prehistoric beasts, like the ichthyosaurus and ***** *********, have laired and copulated and brought forth . . ."

'A motor-bus roared by, like a fabulous noisy red ox with fiery eyes and a luminous interior, quenching his words.

'"Eh?" said Mr Upjohn. "*****!"'

I end quote, feverishly tugging at my beard as if the secret might be hidden therein. What *is* the naughty prehistoric beast, and what is the rude five-letter word forced from Mr Upjohn's lips by the motor-bus?

And try this for size:

'All these things, great fun in themselves, were so much more fun because Priscilla was there, because they held hands and kissed, and felt very serious, like real lovers. ********* ** ***** ** ***** *** ******** *******. And the feeling of friendliness from the clasp of Priscilla's hands, the pleasure of her short, childish kisses and sweet breath, *** ******** ******* ** *** **** ********_******** *******, never quite left him; and to remember Priscilla was like remembering a fragrant English garden.'

End quote, and sluice mouth out with soapy water.

Do you feel that you wish to know more of Priscilla's claspings? Do you want to know more fully what precisely never quite left him? After her short, childish kisses and that breath of hers he liked, it becomes one of the world's longest crossword clues: 'Something filthy in 1929 (3, 8, 7, 2, 3, 4, 8-8, 7).'

I will admit that, working on the 'fragrant English garden' line, I got quite excited when I thought the 8-8 might be 'croquet-mallet'. Then I realised it was 7-6, but while contemplating this shameful, if unforgettable, use of the implement, it occurred to me that the exercise was making a mockery of the whole point of asterisks.

The point is further made by the Chinese edition of *Lady Chatterley's Lover.* In this the censor in his wisdom has had all the saucy moments retained, but in English.

'Censored songs' forms one of the most jovial rounds on radio's *I'm Sorry, I Haven't A Clue,* a strange anti-quiz in which I appear, with Graeme Garden, Tim Brooke-Taylor, Barry Cryer, and Humphrey Lyttleton in the chair. In this, by simply pressing a buzzer judiciously instead of singing the actual word or words of a song, you can render them all quite smutty beyond.

For instance, here's a song previously thought clean as Whistler's Mother but, subjected to this treatment, it can take on, particularly in the battle-scarred voice of Maurice Chevalier, a whole new meaning:

'Each time I see a little girl of
    five or six or seven
I can't resist the joyous urge to *(bleep!)*
    and say
Thank heaven for little girls.'

Was it old Polonius, his voice strangely muffled by the thick curtains over the arras, who said 'There is nothing, either good or bad, but thinking makes it so.' No, it was Hamlet. So true anyway. You can come out now, old fellow. No you can't. Another fine example of gratuitous Shakespearian violence.

THE AGE OF CHIVALRY

Chivalry is now reckoned to be stone-cold dead in de market-place, and this probably *can* be blamed on our times. There's nothing more discouraging for a gentleman of the old school than to open a door at Harrods for a lady and find himself flattened against the wall by a streaming horde of tourists and shoppers with nary a word of thanks between the lot of them. Stop at a zebra crossing, or even *for* a zebra crossing, and horns blare and abuse is hurled. Queueing has become a thing of the past. No one apologises any more or raises a hat. We've become a churlish lot. I blame town planners and architects, traffic wardens, Arabs, metrication and the Common Market.

I remember going into a New York bar years ago. 'Good evening', I said, oozing charm. 'Could I have a beer, please?' The barman looked at me as though I had just presented him with a long-dead lizard. He looked me up and down with obvious distaste. 'What', he grunted, 'is a bierpliz?' I learnt the system in no time: thump a fist on the bar and snap curtly 'Beer!' or 'Scotch!' I felt, though, that something inside had died. It's no different in Britain these days. Mine hosts aren't bluff any more. They wear suits.

And yet one is led to imagine that once upon a time there was this golden age of chivalry, when knights in white satin galloped on their chargers, flinging open doors at Harrods for damsels in distress; slew dragons without batting an eye; slew each other with extreme politeness; always had a 'please' and a 'thank you' and all played with a straight bat. They'd go off to battle for God, Willy, Willy, Harry, Ste, Harry, Dick, John, Harry III and England, with their lodestar's favour – a handkerchief or sock – tied to their lance.

And yet again, when I think of the clanking chevaliers, I think of King Arthur – who was sadly cuckolded by a Frog – and of chastity-belts: man's greatest display of piggery. Apart from which, their table-manners were shocking, and they smelt.

Now you can blame militant feminists to some extent for confusion over door-opening. Is it a sexist act to offer a lady a seat in a crowded Underground? Is it male chauvinism to refuse to let her kiss you on your first date? (Dear Forum, do people still date? Is there still heavy petting? And is there crumpet still for tea? Am I getting old?) But you can't blame feminists for revolting against the chastity-belt; well, not the chastity-belt *per se* – fat chance you'd have these days of clapping the little woman into the ironwork prior to a dirty mid-week at the National Exhibition Centre – but against its successors, the hoover and the eye-level grill. The one sadness I can detect in the levelling of the sexes is the long farewell to chivalry. Faced with dragons, reluctant Georges will snarl 'Kill the bugger yourself' at their fair ladies in distress, hand over an aerosol and return to the sporting print.

Q 'Oh, what can ail thee, Knight-at-Arms, Alone and palely loitering?'

A 'A short-sighted vasectomist'.

THE VIRGIN QUEEN

I've no idea why this leapt to mind, but did you know that the Mr Gillette, famous – but not in our house – for his razor blades, enjoyed the singular Christian names of King Camp? But I digress . . . .

Now that the lengthy search for a Virgin Future Queen is over and done with, it's quite a relief to find oneself back in the days of Good Queen Bess. My word, Mistress Whitehouse would have hated Will Shakespeare. If she and her Bristolians sat through his Collected Works, jotting down all mentions of sex within and sex without of, and violence, gratuitous or not, and racy language, then, upon my sainted Samuel, their abaci and mini-computers would be white-hot and whistling. All this, and the fact that he was supremely popular among the groundlings. There seems to be no record, however, of any weirdo tottering out of the pit after *Richard III* with an irresistible urge to shove his brother into a butt of malmsey wine, or leaving *King Lear* with his thumbs itching to out a few vile jellies. The fact that the Bard was not only relevant to his time, but can still be performed in 'modern dress' – indeed, *The Tempest* has been filmed as a space fantasy – proves the point that man doesn't change. Only the fixtures and fittings do.

And don't worry about the sex and violence, Mistress W – it isn't real. Take the violence. The blood is tomato ketchup or the happily-named Kensington Gore. The 'vile jelly' is, in all probability, vile jelly. It's only real blood on news programmes. The corpses at the end of *Hamlet* are no more lifeless than your Druids are violated, and will be bowing happily with no discomfort at the curtain call. The point of violence in my book is that it must be seen to hurt, otherwise a totally erroneous view of its

beastly nature is given. I remember being told by a BBC producer – who had been seconded to, I think, Tunisian television to help out with its birth and early weaning – of the locals' strict attitude to violence. For instance, take the traditional Western saloon scene: the cast assembled round the poker table, a number of aces tumbling of a sudden from the Missouri gambler's lacy cuffs, our hero leaping to his feet, eyes akimbo . . . then the Tunisians would insert the scissors. Spared from the shock-horror of the gunfight, the next shot the puzzled audience would glimpse was of the gambler staggering through the swing-doors and collapsing, clasping his stomach, in the middle of Main Street. Food poisoning perhaps? An excess of pork and beans? The debate probably still rages.

The other side of the coin is to see Burt Reynolds, after being kneed vigorously in the goolies by a giant of a man who clearly knows his business, spring easily to his feet again, leap over roofs and casually beat the hell out of his assailant. Nothing can encourage violence more than the suggestion that it is painless. If violence is necessary in some piece, then better that ketchup and jelly fly and people are broken and bent, as in life, than that they play some pathetic pat-a-cake, pat-a-cake ballet, breaking balsa-wood chairs with their bare forearms and shaking off the effects of a bottle broken over their heads as if they had been lightly swatted with a small fish. It may not be real, but let it appear to be real. This is what we call acting. Christmas after Christmas, or so it seemed, I used to give my Squire Trelawney in the Mermaid Theatre's *Treasure Island.* Despite killing pirates twice nightly and three times on Saturday, not once was I done for

I'll tell you this for nothing — I am getting jolly fed up with nasty vicious psychos telling me "God told me to do it". This is (a) bloody unlikely and (b) causes a lot of agonising round at the Festival of Light. You will in future blame the Television Set like everyone else. Bring back Hanging, Goodnight and God bless!

GBH. At the same time, if we hadn't gone for each other like tigers, the kids would have hissed and booed and gone back to reading the *Financial Times.*

As I write, almost every film in London seems to be advertised with the gleaming blade of a knife or an axe. Chill hands clutch my bowels when sharp implements are produced on screen. I screamed in *Psycho,* but that is a branch of entertainment. You don't go to *Macbeth* and expect to see the Thane and his ambitious missus singing and dancing gaily to *Isn't It a Lovely Day to be Caught in the Rain?*

SIMULATION/ STIMULATION

The same goes for sex. It may seem rather obvious but the act itself, when performed on film, stage or television, is in fact being acted, not actually performed. In blue movies or in live sex shows they are not acting, they are at it. *In flagrante depicto.* You are enjoying, or not enjoying at all, a hastily organised gang-bang shot in murky light on Super-8 film; you are catching a live action replay as it happened. In the movies proper or on the box, they will represent this, perform it as per the script for some dramatic reason, but they do not actually indulge in it otherwise the time and money wasted after blowing take one ('Hair in the lens!') and take two, while our hero is re-motivated, would be prohibitive.

How far they pretend to go is largely dependent upon the audience they're after. How much they leave to our imagination is entirely in their hands. Chances are that, if two persons vanish behind the sofa, cooing sweet somethings and reading each other in Braille, we all know what will happen next. Whether we are told or not is entirely up to the author, director, producer, film censor, etc. From my own experience when I was in the Army in 1956 or so, and almost nightly attended movies lovingly provided by the Army Kinema Corps, the lads definitely wanted to witness more than Rock Hudson and Doris Day were prepared to demonstrate. 'Get stuck in, Rock!' and 'Get 'em off, Doris!' we would cry at moments of deep

tenderness. It beat church parade, anyway.

The only time I was ever moved to make smoke in a cinema was as an innocent lad on my first visit to Paris. My eyeballs steamed up, my feet kept lifting off the carpet and I lost an old and valued fountain-pen in my excitement. *Les Amants* it was, made by Louis Malle and starring Jeanne Moreau. To the strains of the Brahms String Sextet No. 1 in B Flat played at 16 rpm, Ms Moreau and a Frenchman whose name I forget roamed by moonlight the gardens of a country-house. Leisurely it was, in the finest traditions of French Cinema, but you knew there was going to be a torrid climax. It was the erotic equivalent of watching a well-judged custard-pie routine. By the time they reached the bedroom, many of us had forgotten how to breathe.

Tenderly the top half of Ms Moreau was laid naked across the screen. Here it comes, you thought. She looked suitably pleased. Where was *he?* Ah, those days of innocence, what a waste of time. He'd disappeared out of shot. And yet she still looked pleased; indeed, more pleased every moment. He should be joining in, I thought. She's started without him. What was happening was, of course what the British censor John Trevelyan later described as 'clear implications of cunnilingus which we regarded as censorable'. How boring! As I recall, Ms Moreau and the French gentleman then had a bath together and it cooled us all off. 'Very French!' we all agreed, beaming like Cheshire cats, as we burst from the cinema onto the Champs Elysées in search of cold beer. Funnily enough, we all felt the better for it.

It's amazing to think that, as she lay there seeming to revel in the pleasure of it all, she was probably thinking, 'I shouldn't have had that final Drambuie last night. I must admit I don't fancy our leading man. I wonder if he's *un fruit.* If they insist on take *vingt-sept,* I shall resign. I wonder if I left *le gaz* on?' What an actress! Funnily enough, the poster for the movie couldn't have been more tasteful. They used Rodin's *Le Baiser,* which was refused admittance to the Underground by London Transport. It makes you weep. In their constant search for an agreeable definition for 'obscenity', perhaps they might contemplate the difference between fact and fiction.

MY FIRST AND LAST SCREEN KISS

In 1962 or thereabouts, I composed this rather good joke, I thought, for *That Was The Week That Was.* It was clearly an excerpt from the new wave of British films and went thus: couple grunting, groaning and obviously engaged in sweaty foreplay and weighty petting. As music soars, cut, as they ever did, to every cliché known to cinéastes: expresses racing by, trees falling, huge chimneys collapsing, windows bursting open, storms breaking, lightning and finally great waves crashing on craggy rocks. Then, as ever, we cut back to the bedroom. Wet through and panic-stricken, the man cowers under the bed.

Man: Every time we try anything, that bloody lot happens!

(Applause. Applause. And back to David Frost in the studio.)

All well and good, thought I, until I found myself cast as the threshing gentleman. I was at once the victim of grave doubts. Would I be able to control myself in the clinches ahead? Could I prevent the old Adam from erupting in a shower of fig-leaves? Would I retain my personal freshness under the arc lamps? Would there be loud innuendo re the halitosis? Would the old ticker stand it?

When I heard that I was to be playing this torrid moment opposite Barbara Evans – a lissome brunette, actress, chanteuse and dancer, who would cause the Pope himself to contemplate fresh job opportunities – I realised that the answer to all these questions was probably 'No'. Long had I admired her from afar, but our previous intimacy had been confined to civil 'Good morning's and short exchanges about the cold front approaching from the north-west. Now I was to be clambering about her, hot fronted from the deep south, laying sweaty palms and trembling lips upon her. It was all my springtimes at once, and yet

a young man's fancy turned at once to getting a doctor's note.

We assembled at dawn in a small upper room in Soho. The temperature under the arc lamps was some ten degrees up on that in which Sadie Thompson wove her spell round missionaries and clerical gentlemen in the Pacific. My shirt turned to blotting-paper. I began to check surreptitiously for sudden mustard and cress under my arms. At the director's behest, Barbara and I climbed onto a creaking bed and I lowered myself upon her, while trying not to breathe in her direction, and mopping my brow on a pillow when she wasn't looking. I suddenly found myself thinking that the basic problems of acting spring not so much from the spoken word as from the bits in brackets. Had I not written *(Couple in bed, writhing)* and instead put *(Couple on top of Beachy Head, writhing)* at least there would have been a light breeze, and a possibility of showers. If I'd put *(Tall, dark, handsome person starts to grope lady)* instead of avoiding extra typing and simply putting *(Man),* I'd still be in bed. At home. Would I ever see it again? She was in a racy black peignoir and my left arm was coming out in sympathy with my over-stout heart.

Men with light-exposure meters and measuring tapes hovered about us, whispering the jargon of their trade. Focus-pullers discussed zooms and pans, while the lighting man cried 'Take that chocolate out of your bottom, Arthur, and put an orange in!' A reference, I'm happy to say, to filters.

It came as something of a relief in later years to discover that Stewart Granger, too, found no joy in that sort of thing and he did a deal more of it than I did. Once, just the once, I was asked. But I got the same reaction as he did: the constant nudges and winks and 'Expect you enjoyed that, eh?' Historically, of course, perhaps I should allow myself a small flush of pride that I was in there groping on the British screen, when groping on the British screen was in its infancy.

CHRISTMAS 1984

I was inspired to write the following verse after coursing through the entertainment guide in pursuit of some family show.

Oh, festive tide! Oh, jovial time!
Extol the joys of pantomime!
Peruse the infants' bulging eyes,
The curtain is about to rise.

The orchestra, all damp with beer,
Has lurched into the overture.
The dusty drapes are dragged apart,
The panto is about to start!
What spectacle! Let cynics wince,
See how the chorus pout and mince.
What ho! The merry villagers are sporting on the Green!
It is the opening number – traditionally clean.

(Enter left a chous line in leaking tights and feathered bonnets. They sing through gritted teeth)

The sun is shining on Jollytime Green! Fa! la! la!
And lads and lasses all gaily convene! Fa! la! la! la!
To mingle and gambol and wrestle and thresh
And sweatily indulge in the sins of the flesh!
Let's all be obscene! Fa! la! la!
On Jollytime Green!

Oh, Pandemonium reigneth! Pray stop the children's ears,
Cover up their little eyes and stifle tiny cheers.
Filthy! Disgusting! Rotten show!
The audience gets up to go
Then, as a man, once more they set –
Hang on, it may get filthier yet.
'Hey, Dad, what's that?' 'That's Idle Jack
Pursuing a nymphomaniac.'
The action now is fast and loose,
The goose has goosed old Mother Goose.
Simple Simon in a hat marked 'dunce'
Is liberating women's fronts.
And up there in the royal box
Three bears molesting Goldilocks.
(The programme says she was last unclad in
The late K. Tynan's *Oh, Aladdin!*
But got this rôle since little Noddy's
Put it round he's anybody's.)
Now here comes Santa. Ho, ho, ho!
Look where he's hung his mistletoe!
Beneath the willows Rat and Badger
Explain the mysteries of flage-
Llation to the puzzled Mole
Who's just enjoyed Toad-in-the-hole.
He's been promoted from First Stoat

To play the Frog in the new *Deep Throat;*
He's kissed and turned into a prince,
And has been in a coma ever since.
But what is that compared to that
Which Dick is doing to his cat?*

* *('Five miles from London', she cries, slapping her ample thigh, 'and not a hint of Pussy!' She heads back to the city in pursuit of a few fat directorships.)*

And upstage right, with trip so airy,
Enters an extremely wicked fairy;
A sad man nowadays because
He's half the woman his father was.
The prince is reviving Sleeping Beauty –
Well beyond the call of duty.
Terry Wogan as Widow Twankey
Is blankety-blanking in his hanky.
But hold! What's this? The transformation!
Dandini's had the operation –
This should be the finale of finales,
Prince Charming reveals enormous charlies
And, stiffened with embalming fluid,
Is calmly buggering a Druid.
With not a blink, in manner bold,
Up spake a precocious eight-year-old:
'That boring bird and the lady in tights,
Will they now indulge in Sapphic rites?
This really is a turgid orgy;
We saw it all in *Sister Georgie.*
Apropos of little in particular,
Why did you take Mummy to *Caligula?*
Still, if that's what pleases you adults . . .'
And back he went to the racing results.

The moral of this story, if moral is the word,
Is that adults, unlike children, should be obscene, but not absurd.

THE BRITISH IN INDIA

We British are a very peculiar race. Particularly abroad. And there is no greater student of and commentator upon our larger – and indeed smaller – lunacies both at home and away than James Cameron. I was highly delighted, therefore, while thinking I really should do something about *The Kama Sutra,* illustrated perhaps with some studies from those wondrous piles of erotica at Khajaraho, to come across a fascinating reference to them in his second book of autobiography, *An Indian Summer.* I was amazed to read that the Taj Mahal, far from being a source of national pride and popular song, is in fact extremely offensive to a large number of Indians. It represents to them a blatant advertisement of Mogul domination. Classical Hindu art, which was warm and sexy, charming and explicit (the carvings at Khajaraho are, in the words of a friend of Mr Cameron, 'an enormous stone fucking textbook, a manual of sexual acrobatics'), was viewed by the Moguls as grotesque and they knocked down as much as they could. When India gained independence, the same gentlemen who had banned kissing on the movie screen made a move to wipe out Khajaraho, but they could see it was a tourist-puller. The wondrous statues, entwined in every posture ever attempted by the honest sexual adventurer, therefore remain in the same spot they've occupied for over a thousand years.

The Moguls were Islamic and their artists were not allowed a crack at bodies; not so the Hindus, who chipped away night and day at little else. How their models retained those intricate poses for long without suffering terminal cramps only adds to their mystery. Nevertheless, on reading Mr Cameron, you can understand why Hindus have little time for the antiseptically proper though admittedly beautiful Taj. As he says: 'Representations of the Taj Mahal travel the world on picture postcards; accurate photographs of the carvings of Khajaraho would be seized by the Customs.'

It was extraordinary how *The Kama Sutra* sold like hot beds when it first hit the streets in 1963. There are books, I'll admit, that I've bought in the heat of their publicity and never got past page 27, viz *Dr Zhivago, The Day of the Jackal* (and some I would never buy but have thumbed through at W. H. Smith and *still* never made it past page 27, viz *The Country Diary of an Edwardian Lady*), and I admit *The Kama Sutra* was another, though I have dipped. It certainly can't be recommended as a bedside book: you might well be tempted in the night to have a crack at the Congress of the Screech-owl (page 28). This has been known to lead to an early grave. The book was bought, I imagine, by people who thought, quite genuinely, that it might broaden their sex lives. Even in 1963 there was not much accurate information to be obtained. There was, however, a deal of confusion to be obtained from *The Kama Sutra of Vatsyayana.* It was an encyclopaedia of useless information.

BEST, I THINK, PRESS ON TO PAGE 87, DEAR

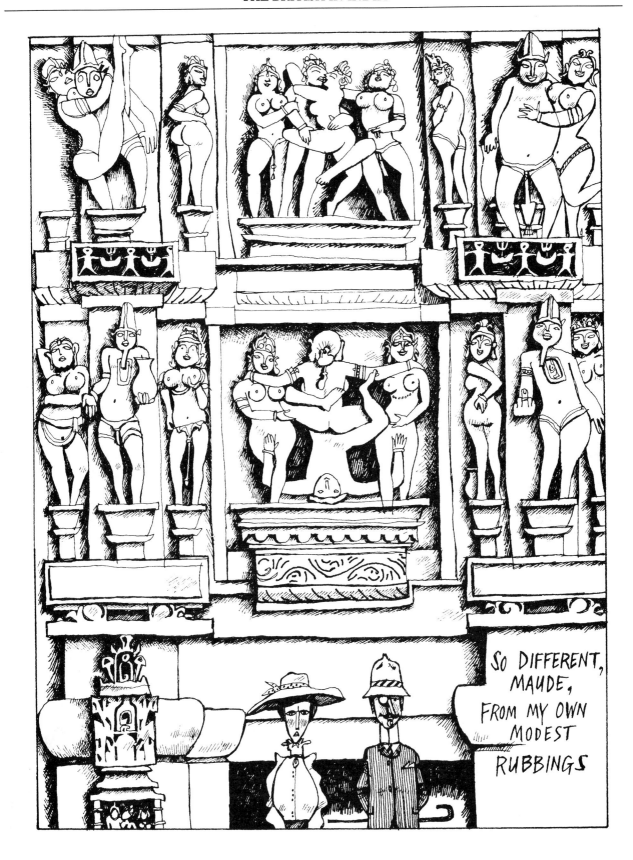

I met this girl at a party in 1964 and, desperate for some conversational gambit, plucked *The Kama Sutra* from the fag-laden air. Had she read it? I enquired.

She: I am a keen student of it. I have studied singing, music, dancing, tattooing, fixing stained glass into the floor, making beds, playing the musical glasses, storing and accumulating water in aqueducts and cisterns and colouring teeth, garments, hair, nails and bodies.

Rushton: *(for want of anything better to say)* I say!

She: Where I fall down is on the binding of turbans, the art of making ear-ornaments, making parrots out of yarn, mimicry, drawing inferences, treating the diseases of trees, teaching starlings to speak and knowledge of the art of war.

Rushton: Well, I have some knowledge of the latter and I can draw an inference. You seem . . . almost perfect. *(Swallows stuffed olive.)*

She: You're not a leper, lunatic, ascetic, extremely white, extremely black, bad-smelling, wife of a relation, friend, learned Brahman or the king?

Rushton: I'm not married at all. Would you like a tender ear of corn?

She: You have read it as well.

Rushton: I have dipped. It's like throwing one wood apple against another. I think.

She: Are you the hare man, the bull man or the horse man?

Rushton: Horse-ish.

She: Bully for you. I'm a female elephant. What's your passion rating?

Rushton: *(modestly)* Middling.

She: I am intense.

Rushton: *(quickly)* Middling to intense.

She: *(clearly besotted)* Shall we sing? Either with or without gesticulations.

Rushton: I beg your –

She: Play on a musical instrument? Talk about the arts?

Rushton: *(remembers moment from his dipping)* Persuade each other to drink? *(He fetches further gins. She sings a snatch of* If I Had a Hammer *– a popular tune at the time.)*

She: You should now be overcome with love and desire.

Rushton: Indeed I am.

She: Then you should dismiss the people that be with you, giving them flowers, ointments and betel-leaves. Meanwhile, I shall carry on amusing conversation and talk suggestively. Perhaps we should go out on to the balcony?

Rushton: Have you got a lingam on you?

(They wander out onto the balcony.)

She: I am going to strike you with passion on the head and the back with the open palm of the hand. Now I can thunder as I do so, or make the sound 'Hin'.

Rushton: 'Hin'?

She: Or, if you'd rather, 'Phût' or 'Phat' – that's an imitation of a bamboo being split. I can say 'Plat'. Or, conversely, I can coo or weep.

The Congress of the SLOTH.

The Congress of the MAD DOG.

The Congress
of the
CUCKOO.

The Congress
of the
RABBIT. Adopting the LETTUCE Position.

The Congress of the SPERM-WHALE.

Rushton: *Chacun à son coo.* If I remember aright you could say 'Mother' as you –

She: Mother! *(Hits him on head vigorously. He savours the moment as if wine tasting.)*

Rushton: *(mildly concussed)* Not really me, that.

She: Can you make a sound like a green pigeon, a bee, a flamingo or a quail?

Rushton: A bee, certainly. Buzz! Buzz! *(She hits him again with back of hand.)*

She: Thus says Suvainanabha: 'These different ways of lying down, sitting and standing should be practised in water because it is easy to do so therein'.

Rushton: I can't swim.

She: After the Congress we don't look at each other. We go to the wash-room. You anoint my body with sandalwood ointment and betel-leaves. You embrace me with your left hand. We sit on the terrace. I put my head in your lap, face towards the moon. You say agreeable words.

Rushton: That was very jolly. What fun. That sort of thing?

She: You give me water and gruel and show me the planets.

Rushton: I only know The Plough.

She: That is the end of sexual union.

Rushton: It's vastly over-rated isn't it? *(He makes an excuse and leaves.)*

(Curtains)

EVERYTHING YOU EVER WANTED TO KNOW ABOUT SEX AND NEVER KNEW EXISTED

I am fortunate in having in my possession a splendid book, *Some Jolly Good Tips for the Sexual Athlete, Garnered During a Lifetime's Extremely Active Service on the Indian Front* by Brigadier-General Sir Hesketh Manley-Pulling: explorer, soldier, poet, pioneer of sex education for the Army and right bastard where the ladies were concerned. He was the author of such diverse works as *The Perfumed Gardener, Kama into the Sutra, Maude* and *Beware the Yellow Beryl* (the latter written after a chastening weekend in Bangkok). He also dabbled in military history; many will know his most famous work, *With Kitchener Through Mrs Bradley*. I quote from the introduction to *Some Jolly Good Tips:*

'Holloa, ye pampered jades of Asia. I have long been pressed by lesser men to tell of my love-affair with India. It began with my first taste of water-buffalo vindaloo and of the sultry lips of Vehera Lingam, the exotic temptress from Nepal – land of the monastery bell and the tango. Not for nothing was Vehera known as "The Sweetheart of the Forces", particularly by the Chaplain-General. She certainly destroyed his faith in Western methods, and he foreswore the missionary position forever in one of the most disgusting displays I have ever witnessed in a pulpit.

'For myself, I cannot speak too highly of the niceties, the vagaries and the pleasures of the rich variety of sexual postures and capers to which I was introduced up the Rann of Kutch in 1889. I determined to get these down on paper.'

He was fortunate in that the local district officer moonlighted for the *Illustrated London News,* sending them occasional etchings of skirmishes with tribesmen and ceremonial involving visiting dignitaries. He agreed to assist Sir Hesketh by illustrating the various Congresses. As their models they were fortunate in procuring the services of Mrs Jarvis, the wife of a cavalry vet and anyone's for a pipe of port, and Major E. P. V. Trussblast of the King's Own Kashmiri Scouts, known to his many intimates as 'The Naked Major'.

The book is divided into clear-cut sections, each with graphic titles such as 'Seduction – Some Useful Banter'. He recommends the following for the candlelit supper-table in a private room: '"Your body, madam, is soft as the mustard seed on the verandah; your skin is as fair as the purple lotus in the shops; your hair is perfumed as the lily bud that has freshly burst, alarming a friendly toad. Your yoni I have not yet had the pleasure of meeting . . ." and so on in that vein. While the lady in question is lost in the magic of your verbiage, you may seize the opportunity to surreptitiously tip the contents of a rhinoceros horn over her avocado pear.'

BITING AND PROVOCATIVE NOISES

Sir Hesketh demonstrates the *right* and *wrong* places to bite ladies. Get her slender ankle, for instance, between your teeth and she will be yours. 'It is better to have a pigeon today than a peacock tomorrow.' Do not, however, attempt to bite a woman of Avanti, or indeed kiss her or mark her with your nails, though 'they have a

fondness for various kinds of sexual union'. The women of Malwa, however, thoroughly enjoy embracing and kissing, and are easily won over with a good smack between the breasts and a cry of 'Phût!' 'The women of the Lal country' – and here he quotes directly from *The Kama Sutra* – 'have even more impetuous desire, and make the sound 'Sit!' (See Barbara Woodhouse.)

SHAMPOOING

'Chances are', Sir Hesketh writes, 'that one is on to a good thing if a woman begins to shampoo one's hair. In India this is generally viewed as very much The Thing to Do. It certainly makes it a deal less embarrassing for a lady who has not been formally introduced to make an advance. She simply shampoos the chappie's hair.'

THE EMBRACE

'When a woman, having placed one of her feet on the foot of her lover and the other on one of his thighs, passes one of her arms around his back and the other about his shoulders, makes slightly the sound of cooing and singing, and wishes, as it were, to climb up him in order to have a kiss – it is called an embrace like the climbing of a tree.'

While posing for a study of this with Mrs Jarvis, Sir Hesketh – standing in for the Major who was incapacitated by a night of rupture – fell, with Mrs Jarvis entwined about him, through the billiard-room window. For the rest of his life he was confined to a wheelchair, and Mrs Jarvis refused ever again to venture upstairs, even for Cockburns.

SEXUAL DEVIATIONS

'It was in the September of the same year in which I gave my all for sex education that I received sad news concerning the Chaplain-General. A platoon of sepoys discovered him wandering the old town in corsets and thigh-length fishing boots, his face coated in powder and rouge. He was put on the next boat home; it was the end of him as a man. But, perversely, it was the beginning of a brilliantly successful career for the Right Reverend Brigadier "Bubbles" Hume, the lady with the fine moustaches and fan-dancer extraordinaire.'

A NOTABLE SEXUAL VARIATION

'One of the most ambitious and yet, in my opinion, one of the most gratifying of the variations that I have encountered out here is the Congress of the Mahout. On the back of an elephant. Watch the old girl's eyes light up as you lumber, cooing and hooting, through the bosky jungle. I admit I've also enjoyed some rare moments on the top of a twopenny bus. That's what we mean by sexual variations. Never let 'em know where you'll strike next.'

THE CONGRESS

'1. When the woman has one of her legs placed on her head and the other crossed beneath her and her lover is lying prostrate with arms akimbo – this is called the Congress of the Death-watch Beetle.
2. When the woman is in the Posture of the Laughing Hyena – one leg in a bucket and the other housed in a straw hat – and the lover the while is squatting on top of the tallboy, chances are that two of the pages have stuck together.'

Sir Hesketh concludes his enthralling book thus: 'I have in my life climbed as high as any in man's constant struggle in the conquest of woman. Many have never reached base camp. Others have packed it in on the south col. I struggled on without oxygen or Sherpas. Did I reach the summit? Friend, there is no summit. But I have enjoyed dirty weekends in Shangri-la, and my rude tent was never empty. We are here but once, and there is only one mountain worth climbing. It leads to paradise.'

Sir Hesketh died as he lived, trying to get his left wheel over a princess of the royal blood while shouting 'The spirit is willing, but the bitch won't keep still!' He is buried in the small churchyard of St-Anne-in-the-Wardrobe, Cocks Balding. On top of Mrs Jarvis.

OLIVER CROMWELL, PROTECTOR

The Puritans remind me of what we used to write large on freshly whitewashed lavatory walls: 'Killjoy was here'. After the Civil War, compared to which the activities of Cecil King seem very small beer ('Very small beer, sir, 95p!'), came the Uncivil Wart: Oliver Cromwell, body-servant of a totally humourless God. One of his first acts on taking up the protectorship was to abolish race-meetings because they were a hotbed for Cavaliers, and none the worse for that: the races are the one place I find them tolerable. He also put the kybosh on the theatre. So, too, has Mother Thatcher, with her beastly VAT and loony economics. Oliver's motives were somewhat different: anything that gives pleasure must, by definition, be sinful. There are still Puritans about. Blanket repression is a good deal easier to administer.

At the beginning of the 1950s the only titties allowed on our silver screen were black ones, usually bobbling about in the dance. This simple rule meant that your censor knew precisely where to put the scissors. First sign of a white titty, and – Cut! Lop! Snip, snip, and Bob's your auntie! In the fullness of time, some distant Swedish titties began to appear, the argument being, one presumes, that the Swedes are as renowned for nude, communal bathing as buxom Negresses are for dancing about Maidenform-less. Also they had sub-titles. In turn, these were deemed to make French titties acceptable, the French being as well-known for doing things in bed together with no clothes on as the distant Swedes are for their state of undress. There was a small undercurrent of patriotic feeling stirring in the cits and souks that abut Wardour Street. What of bare British breasts? was the cry. And for inspiration they turned to that supremely ludicrous magazine

Health and Efficiency, the naturist monthly. Those photographed within appeared to have suffered the most appalling privations. The ladies had been shaven to a bleached white triangle and gentlemen, even more alarmingly, were totally emasculated. If this was the price one had to pay to join a nudist colony, it seemed far, far too dear.

However, films of the book began to appear, sporting such titles as *Nudist Paradise, Nudes of the World* and the like. These were supremely harmless home movies of nude people throwing balls to each other, playing tennis and having lunch, and were perfectly acceptable to the censor as long as the naturists remained in their colonies and didn't show us their genitalia. Now you might have thought that the popularity of these films would have led to a nationwide conversion to naturism, but it was not to be. I think we can blame the weather for this.

(Old joke: *First nudist:* How's your bum?
Second nudist: Shut up!
First nudist: So's mine. It must be the cold weather.)

These films saw, in all probability, the first official turn-out of the Dirty Mackintosh Brigade. What goes on under the dirty mackintosh is as dark a mystery as the secret of the kilt, but there was no chance the lads would march off to the nearest nudist colony. Those mackintoshes never come off. They are occasionally opened for the quick flash, but that's about it.

(Second old joke: It's so cold that in the park the flashers are describing themselves.)

Of a sudden, up came a film in which some naturists strayed off the reservation and

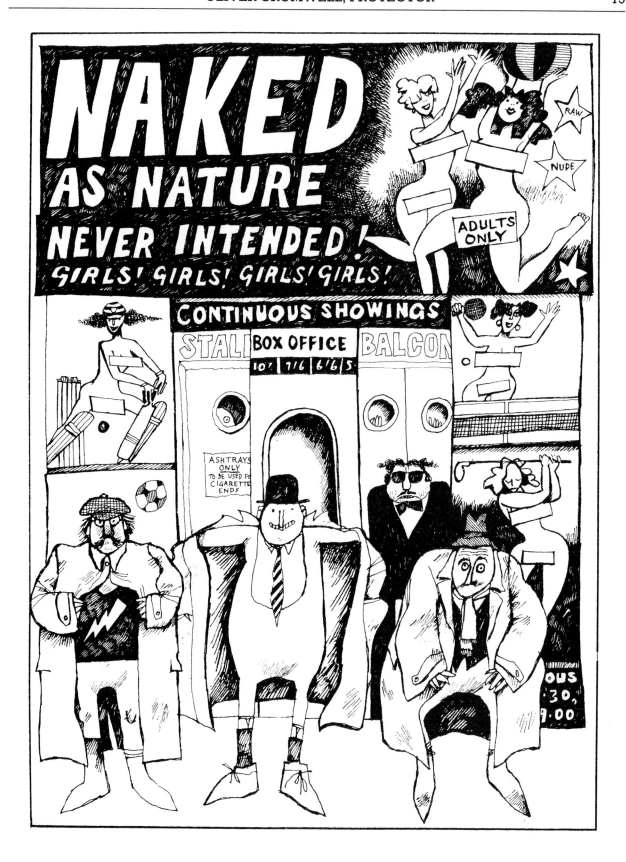

practised their craft on a boat. One also danced. *Sunswept* may well have been a turning-point. The censor's first inclination was to ban it, but he really couldn't see any harm in it, and passed it fit 'For Adults Only'. From that moment, he was forced to ask himself whether a film featuring nude bodies was offensive or not. Isn't total repression simpler? Once you start arguing the pros and cons of allowing a film of two naked people playing ping-pong to be shown or not, all hell is let loose. To assess the height of insanity that can be reached in these matters, thumb through the reports of the *Lady Chatterley* trial. Not only is the prosecution a rare hoot, trotting out 'Would you allow your servants to read this book?' and other famous catch-phrases, but there is the sad spectacle of men of intellect and reason being forced to defend to the death what is ultimately an extraordinarily bad book from a literary point of view. I wonder if anyone reads it any more. You can still make a daisy-chain without embarrassment.

Meanwhile, in the queue outside, the Dirty Mackintosh Brigade were getting restless. They expected more. Quite rightly they were bored far from stiff by naturists playing silly buggers on the verdure. All over Soho, strippers caked in make-up teetered on stiletto heels from basement to basement *(Shows on NOW!)* with their small suitcase and toy poodle. You could hear the rattle of castanets and old bed-springs emanating from Spanish model (second floor).

In 1971 the first shot of an erect penis appeared on our screens in a film from Yugoslavia called W. R. The author would like to point out that the penis in question is fictitious and bears no relation to himself. He has also never been to Yugoslavia.

Very well, one confession for you: I once did a strip-tease for the women's magazine Nova. *(It was shortly after Burt Reynolds had revealed all in* Cosmopolitan.*) I refused to remove my underpants, however; I said that some secrets should remain between their readership and I. They closed an issue later. There's no satisfying some women.*

There was also general resentment at not being allowed to see Brigitte Bardot's bare breasts, a sight freely available to those across the Channel, whereas all we got was the jagged edge of the censor's chainsaw and a jump in the music. Heavens to Betsie, it said 'For Adults Only' outside and they were armed with an 'X' certificate to protect the innocent. I doubt that anyone was ever depraved or corrupted by a view of Miss Bardot's bare bosom. In my view, it wasn't her best bit, but we're all different: a fact that was lost on the Great Protector.

Mr David Elfer, QC, defending Lenk, said the shows were not a great success.

"Mrs Novak went down like a lead balloon," he added.

The jury found all five guilty.

Fining the men £60 each and the women £40 each, Judge Ian Starforth Hill, QC, said: "This jury has fired a broadside salvo across the bows of those ships who are sailing with a striptease flag nailed to the mast.

"If I had not been satisfied the audiences had dwindled and that nobody had made any money from this sort of entertainment, I would have had no hesitation in passing a prison sentence."

SOME CAUTIONARY WORDS OF A MEDICAL NATURE

PENILE INJURIES FROM VACUUM CLEANERS

from the British Medical Journal

Case reports

Case 1—A 60-year-old man said that he was changing the plug of his Hoover Dustette vacuum cleaner in the nude while his wife was out shopping. It "turned itself on" and caught his penis, causing tears around the external meatus and deeply lacerating the side of the glans. The external meatus was reconstructed and the multiple lacerations of the glans repaired with catgut. The final result was some scarring of the glans, but the foreskin moved easily over it.

Case 2—A 65-year-old railway signalman was in his signal box when he bent down to pick up his tools and "caught his penis in a Hoover Dustette, which happened to be switched on." He suffered extensive lacerations to the glans, which were repaired with catgut with a good result.

Case 3—A 49-year-old man was vacuuming his friend's staircase in a loose-fitting dressing gown, when, intending to switch the machine off, he leaned across to reach the plug: "at that moment his dressing gown became undone and his penis was sucked into the vacuum cleaner." Because he had a phimosis he suffered multiple lacerations to the foreskin as well as lacerations to the distal part of the shaft of the penis, including the external meatus. His wounds were repaired with catgut and the phimosis reduced with a dorsal slit.

A doctor writes: This unusual complaint, which seems to be reaching epidemic proportions, explains man's natural fear of the hoover. I myself am quite frankly terrified of launderettes and lawn-mowers for the same reason. These modern aids, from which woman is free of any danger (though I have read of a lady in Reading who suffered an involuntary mastectomy at the hands of a garbage disposal unit) are best avoided by men. I recommend rushing from the house at the sight or sound of any of these appliances. You will find that a large whisky will steady the nerves. She will understand.

FURTHER BAD NEWS FOR WOMEN

Dancers at the Folies Bergère suffer from digestive problems caused by fast food, orthopaedic problems caused by high-kicking, allergies caused by body make-up, insomnia and skin diseases. Apart from which, this notice was discovered backstage at the Raymond Revuebar:

'The impression created by some of you is that you are totally disinterested in what you have just done on stage. It is important at the end of the number to wait for the festoon to be lowered and to smile during the applause.'

And for the spittoon to be brought on.

The "Powermaster" is a precision hand made instrument comprising of three parts (A) Exhaust Pump (B) Perspex Cylinder (C) Rubber Flange.

PENIS EXERCISER AND DEVELOPER

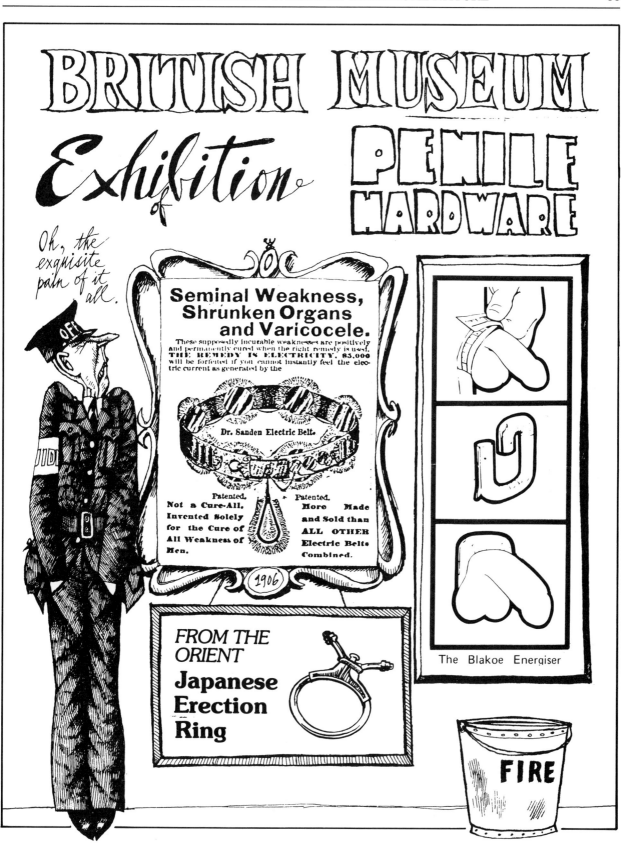

IN GOOD KING CHARLES' GOLDEN DAYS

The royal family, bless it and lang may it reek, has always been in there rooting. The Edwards have been particularly liberated, starting with Edward III, who was quite a lad; the Seventh, of course, a legend in his own time; and the Eighth, whose well-known penchant for married women led to Mrs Simpson. The Georges, with one exception, have been rather reticent and the Williams come last. The overall winners on a head-count are the Charlies, and they owe it all to Charles II. Charles III-to-be, I imagine, has had his moments. I do hope he's had his moments. Admittedly, it would have improved the quality of life if he'd married a thrice-divorced black Catholic.

Charles II, however, certainly made himself accessible. The reason may well have been that his wife, Catherine of Braganza, was not only Portuguese but also suffered from terminal halitosis. Barbara Cartland, who should know, describes him as 'the most gallant, exciting king England ever had' . . . and that Lady Walters ever had . . . and Frances Stuart, Duchess of Richmond . . . and the Duchess of Mazarin . . . and the Duchess of Portsmouth . . . and Lady Barbara Castlemaine . . . and Nell Gwynne, the good old Protestant whore. Mrs Whitehouse wouldn't have liked him either.

Talking of Playboys of the Western World, do you realise that magazine first hit the bookstalls of America in 1953? Hugh Hefner, the Walt Disney of sex, apparently used to get it together on his kitchen table. (Sorry, m'lud, another *lapsus linguae* – the italics are yours.) As far as I can recall, all we had going in Britain was *Diana Dors in 3-D, Laya Raki* (now *there's* a memory), *Lilliput,* a pocket-sized *Men Only,* and *Blighty,* which seemed very sophisticated at the time. In addition, former music halls, like the poor lamented Chelsea Palace, were now turning into strip theatres.

None of that is mentioned in Mother Whitehouse's history of the world, and yet with hindsight you can see the worm turning. Nor indeed is there any mention, and the end is nigh in her chapters on the 1960s, of the emergence of the new subversives. The Royal Court, irate middle-class folk snorting out of *Look Back in Anger* and going back to Ongar, movies like *Room at the Top, Saturday Night, Sunday Morning, A Kind of Loving, A Taste of Honey* (with new, powerful social realism), *Victim* (a homosexual barrister), *No Love for Johnnie* (an adulterous MP), the Establishment Club, *Beyond the Fringe* and *Private Eye:* all these were undermining Mother W's 'accepted values and standards', and why not? We'd all suffered the Second World War, post-war austerity and a decade of Tory rule, so it was high time accepted values and standards *were* reassessed.

In defence of Sir Hugh Carleton-Greene, at whose ample feet the blame of Armaggedon has been laid, let it be said that the BBC never leads. It follows. *TW3* and the new plays the Beeb produced (here she comes again – 'his determination to give the freedom of the screen to the protagonists of the new morality, to open the doors to foul language, blasphemy, excesses of violence and sex') were a natural consequence of what had been going on for some years in the arts generally and life in particular, and few doubted that these moves were in the right direction. (The Profumo Scandal and the Vassall Affair which followed soon after were probably not caused by the influence of television, whatever you may say.)

If these moves were on slightly too elevated an intellectual plane for the Dirty Mackintosh

Mr Samuel Pepys — The Dirty Bits

Brigade, relief for them was on its way. (Hand, £5. Topless hand, £10. A short course of Swedish Army exercises, £20.) Blue movies loomed large in the public eye and in two groups (the pseudo-educational – how to make babies in ninety-three different postures – and the 'It-doesn't-matter-what-they-do-together-as-long-as-it's-in-Swedish' school), and if Soho and other areas of our great nation have taken a pounding as a result of this, don't blame it on Sir Huge. Blame on the local planning persons the fact that traditional French tea-rooms have turned into Danish tarts-parlours, that favourite delicatessens have overnight changed into dark blue movie-houses, and that the wet-fish shop is now a wet dream factory. It's the local authority's fault such things are allowed to flower, multiply and advertise garishly. If the wet-fish shop had suddenly erupted with neon bloaters blazing and strobe-lit sprats dancing in the window, the council would have descended upon them like a ton of pricks. If what has happened to Soho happened to any other village in England, there would be a revolution.

The fact that they stay in business, and indeed proliferate, shows that there must be considerable public demand. From tourists, in the main – the low life is always more tempting abroad. (It's the sub-title sin-drome. It doesn't seem so vile in a foreign tongue, and there's less chance of bumping into the neighbours.) It's not all foreign tourists, however; there are also merry British souls who go to London, and Soho in particular, for a good time. There's a certain sadness in that, but you wonder how many visit more than once. I wouldn't mind not going there again and that saddens me. I liked Soho.

From my observations, I'd say there are only two ways to exit with dignity from a dirty book-shop. The first is to emerge, roaring with laughter and shaking one's head sadly. The other is to leap out of the door at enormous speed and appear suddenly standing on the kerb looking upwards, as if one has just had an amazingly lucky fall from a passing Boeing.

AN INTERESTING QUIZ

Q Put a date on this: 'The recent great increase in juvenile delinquency is, to a considerable extent, due to demoralising cinematograph films.'

A 1911, when film censorship seems to have been in the hands of the Fire Brigade.

Q When did the first naked lady cavort on camera?

A In the 1870s. Edward Maybridge laid out an assault course of trip-wires and box-cameras, and produced the appearance of motion by taking a series of pictures set off by a naked lady of his acquaintance who tripped among the wires.

Q When were the first blue movies shown in Britain?

A In 1908. There is an advert in a *Kinematograph Weekly* plugging 'Very piquant films and lantern slides'. These are recommended as 'Special for Gentleman performances'.

Plus ça change, plus c'est la même 'Shows on NOW!'

THE WAR OF INDEPENDENCE

I think it was very fortunate that we lost to the Americans. They've made much better use of the space. Look how the country grew once we'd left our former colonies on the eastern seaboard; we'd never have got as far as Hollywood and, if we had, it would now be famous for its declining motor car industry. But perhaps the most useful aspect of our loss was that, having set the fashions for so long, there was now someone to follow who spoke the same language. We get their movies, their popular songs and singers, their fast food, their soft drinks, their television detectives, a good deal of their weather, their denim trousers, their missiles and a very good idea of what we'll be doing next.

It was therefore highly alarming on one single day in April to read the two following headlines:

America is fed up with sex

By BRIAN VINE
in NeW York

AMERICANS are turning off sex. According to a

and almost immediately:

Mormon conference attacks homosexuals

From AP
in Salt Lake City

Homosexuality is an acquired addiction" like drugs

tance as a sign their church was led by Jesus Christ and was being fought by " the adversary"

and then fall upon a photograph of Linda Lovelace doing an impersonation of Mrs Whitehouse. My God, what's coming next?

My first thought was that the Mormons were still seeking vengeance upon someone for the unprovoked rape of one of their number and desecration of his sacred undervest by Joyce ('I love him so much I would ski down Mount Everest with a carnation between my nipples' which became 'up my nose' in the bowdlerised version) McKinney. Involving as it did oral sex, bondage, kidnapping and rape, it was a very modern love story. It would make a first-rate musical, although singing might be well-nigh impossible in the big number.

As to America giving up sex, they're suckers for statistics and reports, Kinseys and Masters and Johnsons. In this new study it appears that fifteen per cent of men and twice that number of ladies are undergoing 'moderate to severe aversion to sex'. There is something very strange going on over there although I think it's irrelevant to the aversion to sex – and I would suggest it may have something to do with the Lolita complex. If American films aren't about carving knives, they seem to concern nymphets: Brooke Shields (who sounds like a make of

ATTENTION AGENTS AND STUDIOS

Joyce McKinney, the beauty queen in the "Mormon Kidnap Case," is writing a book and screenplay! This moving love story has taken Britain by storm, invoking front page headlines in all British newspapers. It is a tender, sensitive drama involving love, sex, religion, a beautiful intelligent girl (former "Miss Wyoming World," with PhD.), and a handsome priest (missionary). Due to the overwhelming volume of inquiries by phone (10-20 calls per day), she is forced to look for representation. Legitimate parties please contact by letter only: Joyce McKinney, C/O Stuart Elgrod, Attorney, T.V. Edwards Co., Textile House, 87 High St., Gardiner's Corner, London E1 7QY, England. No more phone calls please!

rubber good), Tatum O'Neal, and Jodie Foster, the girl who allegedly drives men to take potshots at presidents. (There's democracy in action – when every ambitious lad born in the USA can one day have a crack at the president.)

I have a sneaking suspicion that the recent Broadway adaptation of *Lolita* by Edward Albee bombed because the heroine was played by a twenty-four-year-old woman. This is clearly not what the public want. Is Little Orphan Annie a sex-symbol?

No, I fancy what's going on there – and what may well happen here next – is the extraordinary phenomenon of being 'born again'. Religion is now Big Business. All Sunday on every television channel in America are programmes from what seem to be Pedestrian Shows from Earl's Court. These are regaled by some holy heavy, backed by family, full orchestra and chorus, and all clad in white suits and Grecian robes, with an hour and a half of Elmer Gantry.* It is total show-biz, miracles are frequently performed on camera, and cheques – God bless you, send whatever you can – should be made

out to J. Christ and addressed to Madison Avenue. And if you think it couldn't happen here, I should warn you that I saw Billy Graham at Haringay Arena years ago and the effect was shattering. People were even kissing the feet of the solo trombonist.

Even Linda Lovelace, née Boreham, queen of the gamazons, empress of hard porn, appears to have been born again. Gone is the heroine of *Deep Throat* who gaily announced (never speak to the Press with your mouth full): 'I was just playing myself; I was just enjoying myself. I don't consider that a woman is being used by a man ever; she is there to please. I mean, I please, then I'm fulfilled.' Now in her book *Ordeal,* she reveals that all this was said and performed under threat of being shot by her husband. If the queue to shoot Reagan doesn't cause reform in the gun laws, surely this will. At the same time as she professes her innocence, the book gives graphic details of what went on, rather in the style of those newspapers that print pictures of all sorts of things going on behind closed doors with the headline 'Should Children be Allowed To See These Disgusting Scenes?' or such.

I find her old producer, Lou Perry, the most interesting figure. In 1973 he announced, 'I think we will have a three-year span when there'll be a lot of sex-movies, and it will burn itself out'. Ho, ho, ho. He then added that he wanted to make Linda into a female Woody Allen. She has made an even more extraordinary conversion. And great should be the rejoicing round at the offices of the Festival of Light. Religion is the one to look out for, fans! Watch J. R. get it suddenly on *Dallas* – it can be just as loony.

---

* One of the leading Bible-belters, Oral Roberts, runs a religious hour on cable television to 200,000-odd subscribers late at night. Bouncing off an adjacent satellite is a very rude hour of live sex and frolic from New York. One golden night last April, as Oral pronounced 'Something wonderful is about to happen to you', onto his network leapt blue film lasting for a good ten minutes. He received only one complaint.

Q What is wrong with Mrs Whitehouse's following paragraph re the Bishop of Woolwich giving evidence as a defence witness in the *Lady Chatterley* trial?

'Whatever may have been the motivations of the thirty-four other "experts" – theologians, university dons, politicians and assorted "moralists" – who joined the Bishop, no one can rightly judge. But the fact is that, between them, they enabled Penguin Books to sell four million copies of D. H. Lawrence's book and established a major bridgehead for the pornographers.'

A No, they didn't. The prosecution did.

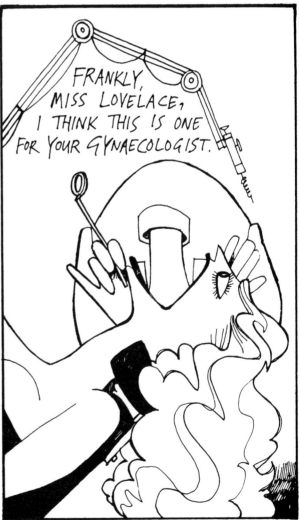

QUEEN VICTORIA DEAD – A NATION MOURNS

June Esserman, an eminently sensible lady, and the big cheese at the Child Research Service in New York, made an interesting point about Popeye. At the moment he is all over the television and cinema screens and the kids love him. Why, then, is spinach not the world's best-selling vegetable? She, in fact, was making a case to prove that children are less susceptible to commercials than parents believe. I think the same may well apply to the programmes. Children don't sit and watch television like adults – they usually lie on the floor with their backs to it and do something else. Admittedly, they are a deal more sophisticated than we were at that age but also, I fancy, wiser.

I'm always a little suspicious when the blame for some juvenile excess is blamed on the box. I read of an American youth who shot his parents and claimed he was deeply under the influence of *Kojak.* Kojak didn't shoot his parents. People who shoot parents on *Kojak* meet sticky ends. Telly Savalas, give him his due, stopped sucking lollipops for fear of being accused of depraving and corrupting young teeth. Mrs Whitehouse makes much of customers being carried out of *The Exorcist,* but she may have swooned as others did when Bing Crosby crooned. Much of this hysteria is caused by the advance publicity: 'You will scream your lungs out at this film', 'Plastic bags are available from the usherettes', 'If you die of shock during this motion picture, we will give your dependants some money' and so on. I remember how we all screamed on cue at Mother's appearance in *Psycho.* Much of it is also caused by the advance brouhaha from the opposition. I remember enjoying *The Devils* and *Rosemary's Baby,* and I quite liked *Straw Dogs.* After all, life isn't all musical comedy. Dancing isn't the only thing to go on in the dark.

And I don't in all honesty believe that life would be better if lived according to Barbara Cartland's romances or the works of publishers Mills and Boon. Yet 100,000 women read each Mills and Boon 187-page book, available at most branches of Tesco and Woolworth. These torrid tales boast craggy-jawed heroes named Jett, Brock, Marsh or Garth who indulge in steamy but non-smutty relationships with lovely creatures called Shona or Gleena or Arwenna. These are written by ladies with equally exotic names like Karen van der Zee or Mary Wibberley. My grandmother lived on light romances. I can still remember the hideous embarrassment I suffered when I was forced to go to the Boots Lending Library in Kensington High Street and, as I was one of the few who could read her writing, having to read out her list of chosen titles to tittering librarians. But then I never understood how people can read westerns. Here are Mills and Boon in action (not personally):

'Her arms opened to his, gathering his muscled torso into her embrace and a muffled groan escaped his throat before his mouth claimed her yielding lips. Her breast swelled as his hand took its weight in his palm. He dragged his mouth from hers, travelled over her cheek to nibble the lobe of her ear. . . .'

Where are you, Mother Whitehouse, at a time like this? You should be bursting through the window with a woolly sock over your head, blasting Jett and Gleena to bits with your elephant-gun. 'Muscled torsos' and 'yielding lips' – how low can you stoop? But I'm not going to start an anti-Mills and Boon league dedicated to saving 100,000 ladies from themselves. Whatever turns them on, is my cry in these dark days. One must bow to public demand which means, presumably, that I mustn't point the finger at Soho, which also satisfies the urges of other members of the public. I might well find myself marching under Mother W's banner were it a march in favour of restoring Soho. Not, may I hasten to add, that there is no place in our society for sex-shops, sex-shows and dirty-bookeries, but I would complain bitterly if any other eight or nine blocks of London were taken over entirely by butchers or greengrocers.

Alas for Mrs Whitehouse, her banner is covered in so many strange devices that any issue raised under it is automatically blurred. It's laughably simple these days to create an outcry. The world seems to be covered in piles of soap-boxes and the rusting wreckage of shattered band-wagons. Mrs Whitehouse's outcries are good space-fillers for the Press, but it's a criminal over-simplification to suggest that all change and decay is caused by films, television and the theatre.

She dedicates her book to six children 'in the faith and hope that they will grow up in a better world'. You can't argue with that, but even in the perfect world there is an under-world and, while we should arm children for the future with love, tolerance, and as much wisdom and wit as we can instil, we should also coach them in the basic technique of using a knuckle-duster.

It's not the fantasy and fiction that cloud a child's mind and cause a rich variety of confusions, it's bleeding life. Sex is not the be-all and end-all. An enormous number of people would rather have a curry, or a game of football, or watch *Tom and Jerry*. (All, some · crackpot will shout, the worst sort of violence. Shut up, crackpot!) But when the kids of today look at what the world has to offer – unemployment, urban rot, housing, terrorism, the Bomb, the PIE, the Third World, the refugee problem

SHALL ONE MILLS & BOON ?

– and are suffering at the same time the old problems that beset all schoolkids – school, home, parents, teachers, bullies, growing up, acne – it's no wonder they feel pressured. You will get VD if you even go to an X-film.

They have a sex education now which we never had; and if it leaves them slightly bewildered at all the fuss, I think *their* children will benefit from it. They'll feel free to discuss their worries with *their* parents, and get a sensible answer. The films shown in schools at the moment are about as much fun as a documentary from New Zealand on the building of a motorway near Auckland. Full-frontal cartoons and shots of breast-feeding and chickens tending their young, plus information on the laying of eggs and, still my old favourite, maps of the backs of rabbits. As they grow older they learn about contraceptives and VD, and have class discussions with Teacher. There's the rub. Teachers can make *history* boring! Why can't it be simply stressed that it isn't all that important? It's fun, but 'O'-levels come first. That it should never be a source of fear, panic and guilt. It's

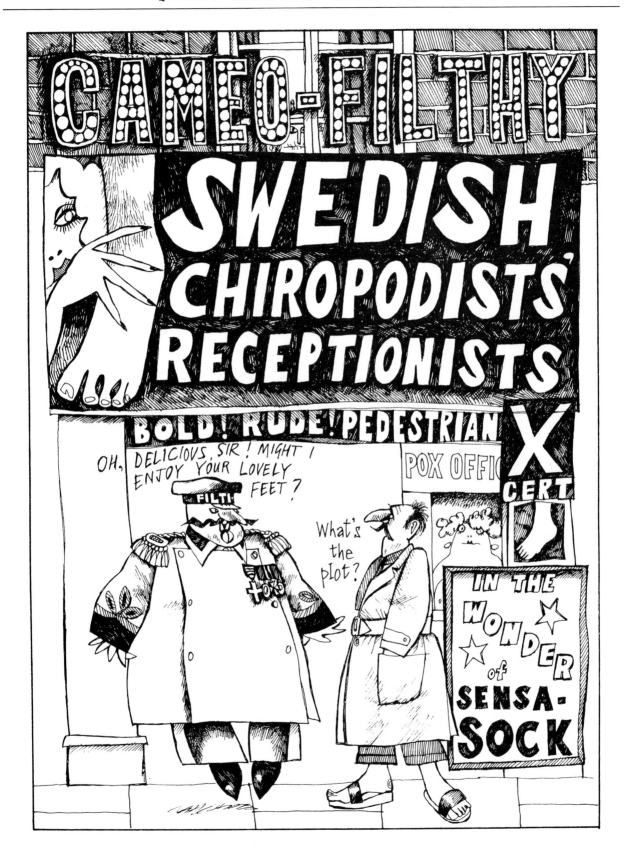

part of life's rich pattern, but only a part.

Mrs W is terrified by the loss of guilt; she feels the floodgates would open. A loss of guilt doesn't necessarily mean a loss of innocence. The loss of virginity doesn't mean you are morally obliged to regret it in the morning, or that you are instantly awarded adulthood, and should sign up at once, shameless hussy, with a Maltese pimp.

If only Mrs Whitehouse had remained a schoolteacher, and aimed for fewer targets instead of blanket-bombing a piece of Dresden. A little laughter is a lot more useful than prudish hectoring and badgering. But she has the whiff of gunsmoke in her nostrils and any moment now will march on Moscow, the Napoleon of Prurience. It must have come as a fearful shock to her system when Larry Lamb was knighted for services to *The Sun,* and she only got the CBE. But that's the way of it. There is, thank the Lord, rough justice. Ho, ho ho, *He* has a sense of humour.

The nice June Esserman also said, 'If you live by the ocean, it's wiser to teach your child to swim than to try to build a fence around the sea'. You should also warn them politely of the perils of sharks and jellyfish and the pleasures of making sand-castles, and encourage them to search the rocks for shells and interesting flotsam and to avoid the daft old bat who roams the pier shouting about the vile implications of the Punch and Judy show. You're quite right, Ms Esserman. I shall sit on this rock and ask myself whatever happened to paddling?

WHATEVER HAPPENED TO HEAVY PADDLING?